CW00558064

POMONA BRITANNICA

George Brookshaw

POMONA BRITANNICA

The Complete Plates | Die vollständigen Tafeln | Les planches complètes

TASCHEN

KÖLN LONDON MADRID NEW YORK PARIS TOKYO

ACKNOWLEDGEMENTS

The copy used for printing belongs to the Staatliche Bücher- und Kupferstichsammlung Greiz/ Thuringia. We thank Gotthard Brandler and the libraries' employees for their friendly assistance. Thanks are due to Edwin Paas for the recipe selection in this volume.

DANKSAGUNG

Der Druck erfolgte nach dem Exemplar in der Staatlichen Bücher- und Kupferstichsammlung Greiz/Thüringen. Wir danken Gotthard Brandler und den Mitarbeitern der Bibliothek für die freundliche Unterstützung.
Dank gebührt auch Edwin Paas für die Auswahl der Rezepte des vorliegenden Bandes.

REMERCIEMENTS

L'impression a été effectuée d'après l'exemplaire de la Staatliche Bücher- und Kupferstichsamm-lung Greiz/Thüringen. Nous remercions Gotthard Brandler et le personnel de la bibliothèque pour son aimable soutien.
Nous tenons également à remercier Edwin Paas pour la sélection des recettes sur cet ouvrage.

Project management: Petra Lamers-Schütze, Cologne
Editorial coordination: Thierry Nebois, Leslie Weißgerber, Cologne
Photographs: Christoph Schmidt, Berlin
Botanical editing: Walter Hartmann, Hohenheim
English translation: Ann Hentschel, Göttingen
French translation: Anne Charrière, Croissy-sur-Seine
Design: Claudia Frey, Cologne
Cover design: Angelika Taschen, Cologne
Production: Ute Wachendorf, Cologne

Printed in Germany
ISBN 3-8228-1463-6

CONTENTS

Inhalt | Sommaire

POMONA BRITANNICA
A masterpiece of pomology | Ein Meisterwerk der Pomologie | Un chef d'œuvre de la pomologie

Allegory of Horticulture, 1769
A. L. Wirsing, copperplate engraving after a drawing by S. Wale

Putti with a garland of flowers and fruits are hovering above Pomona, the Roman goddess of fruits and gardening. She is holding open her robe to catch the fruits tumbling out of the ample cornucopia. She is sharing with the orchard growers, whose tools are now lying idle, the happy occasion of a rich harvest.

Allegorie auf den Gartenbau, 1769
A. L. Wirsing, Kupferstich, nach einer Zeichnung von S. Wale

Putti schweben mit einer Girlande aus Blumen und Früchten über Pomona, der römischen Göttin der Früchte und des Obstbaus. Sie breitet ihr Manteltuch aus, um die aus einem prall gefüllten Horn herausfallenden Früchte aufzufangen. Das freudige Ereignis einer reichen Ernte teilt sie mit den Obstgärtnern, deren Arbeitsgeräte nun ruhen.

Allégorie de l'horticulture, 1769
Gravure sur cuivre de A. L. Wirsing, d'après un dessin de S. Wale

Des putti volètent en tenant une guirlande de fleurs et de fruits au-dessus de Pomona, déesse romaine des fruits et de la culture fruitière. Elle déploie les pans de son manteau pour recueillir les fruits qui tombent d'une corne d'abondance remplie à ras bord. Avec les jardiniers, elle partage la joie d'une récolte abondante. Les outils sont au repos.

Pomology – The science of fruits

Today virtually everyone knows the names of the common and popular apple varieties, such as Golden Delicious and Granny Smith. But this has not always been the case. By the end of the 18th century thousands of different varieties of fruits were being cultivated, yet horticulturists and hobby gardeners had very little information about them. Knowing their names and other scant details was not enough to distinguish with certainty between the individual varieties. One consequence of this was that among the countless varieties of English apples a single variety could be known by several names – and these names differed not just from county to county, but even between neighbouring towns. Older fruit varieties were continually being reintroduced under different names and proclaimed as new strains of improved quality. Even inferior varieties resembling cultivated stocks were successfully passed off as the better-quality fruits. To make some sense of this confusion a special branch of botany was developed in the 18th century. It is referred to as experimental pomology. This study of fruit growing and the different varieties was the first stage of the science of pomology, which only established itself in the second half of the 19th century. Not only horticulturists and nurserymen but also hobby gardeners and fruit lovers focused on describing, identifying and systematically classifying the various kinds of fruits. Books about fruit farming presented both established and new varieties in words and pictures (ill. 1). More specialized works on fruit varieties also emerged, which are referred to as pomonas. With the dawning of the 19th century came a blossoming of elaborately illustrated pomological print editions. The *Pomona Britannica* by George Brookshaw (published in 1812) is the most comprehensive English publication and its hand-coloured prints are regarded as among the best ever made.

George Brookshaw's life and work

The Englishman George Brookshaw was born in Birmingham in 1751 and died in Greenwich near London in February 1823. Very little is known about his childhood, youth and training; nor is much known about his later life. Not even a portrait of him has survived. It is entirely possible that Brookshaw received instruction in art from his brother Richard Brookshaw (1736– c. 1804), who was an engraver by profession. Richard was particularly well versed in the printing techniques of mezzotint and copperplate engraving – his engraved portraits after paintings by other artists made his name known beyond the British Isles. At the close of the 18th century he was even able to establish himself in Paris as a copperplate engraver.

Pomologie – Die Wissenschaft vom Obst

Heute kennt fast jeder die Namen gängiger und beliebter Apfelsorten wie Golden Delicious und Granny Smith. Aber das war nicht immer so: Obwohl bis zum Ende des 18. Jahrhunderts Tausende von verschiedenen Obstsorten kultiviert wurden, wussten Gärtner und Gartenliebhaber über sie jedoch nur wenig. Die bloßen Namen und geringfügige zusätzliche Informationen waren unzureichend, um mit Sicherheit die einzelnen Sorten unterscheiden zu können. Dies führte zum Beispiel in England bei den unzähligen Apfelsorten dazu, dass eine Sorte unter mehreren Namen bekannt sein konnte – und zwar nicht erst in benachbarten Grafschaften, sondern bereits in Nachbarorten. Ältere Obstsorten wurden unter verschiedenen Namen wiederholt eingeführt und als neue Sorten mit verbesserter Qualität proklamiert. Es war sogar möglich, minderwertige Sorten, die den qualitativen Züchtungsergebnissen ähnlich sahen, als sehr geschätzte Früchte auszugeben.

Um dieser Verwirrung Herr zu werden, entwickelte sich im Verlauf des 18. Jahrhunderts eine botanische Spezialdisziplin: die so genannte experimentelle Pomologie. Diese Lehre vom Obstbau und den Obstsorten bildete die Vorstufe der wissenschaftlichen Pomologie, die sich erst ab der zweiten Hälfte des 19. Jahrhunderts etablierte. Vor allem Gärtner und Baumschulgärtner, aber auch Garten- und Obstliebhaber konzentrierten sich auf die Beschreibung, Bestimmung und systematische Einteilung der verschiedenen Obstsorten. In Büchern über den Obstbau wurden bewährte und neue Sorten in Bild und Wort vorgestellt (Abb. 1). Andererseits entstanden spezielle Werke über Obstsorten, die als „Pomonas" bezeichnet werden. Seit dem Beginn des 19. Jahrhunderts gipfelte die Blütezeit der pomologischen Tafelwerke in prächtigen Druckausgaben: Die *Pomona Britannica* von George Brookshaw (erschienen 1812) ist die umfangreichste englische Publikation und die kolorierten Farbdrucke zählen zu den Hochwertigsten, die je geschaffen wurden.

George Brookshaws Leben und Werk

Der Engländer George Brookshaw wurde 1751 in Birmingham geboren und starb im Februar 1823 in Greenwich bei London. Über seine Kindheit, Jugend und Ausbildungszeit wie auch sein späteres Leben ist nur wenig bekannt; ein Porträt von ihm ist nicht überliefert. Es ist durchaus möglich, dass Brookshaw eine künstlerische Ausbildung durch seinen als Kupferstecher tätigen Bruder Richard Brookshaw (1736– um 1804) erhielt. Letzterer war vor allem in den Drucktechniken Mezzotinto und Kupferstich versiert – nicht nur auf den Britischen Inseln machte er sich mit gestochenen Porträts nach Gemälden anderer Künstler einen

La pomologie ou la science des fruits

De nos jours, qui ne pourrait citer quelques noms de variétés courantes de pommes, agréables au palais, telles que la Golden Delicious ou la Granny Smith? Mais il n'en a pas toujours été ainsi. Même si des milliers de variétés de fruits étaient cultivés à la fin du XVIIIe siècle, les jardiniers professionnels et amateurs ne savaient que peu de choses à leur sujet. Le seul nom, complété par quelques indications sommaires, ne suffisait pas à les distinguer avec précision les unes des autres. En Angleterre, par exemple, où il existait d'innombrables variétés, il n'était pas rare que l'une d'entre elles changeât de nom d'un comté à l'autre, voire d'un village à l'autre. Des variétés plus anciennes, réintroduites sous des noms différents, étaient présentées comme une sorte nouvelle, dont on vantait la qualité améliorée. Il était même possible de faire passer des fruits médiocres pour des produits très appréciés, lorsqu'ils ressemblaient à des variétés de qualité, obtenues par culture.

Afin de mettre de l'ordre dans cette confusion, une discipline spécifique se développa au cours du XVIIIe siècle: la pomologie dite expérimentale. Cette connaissance de la culture du fruit et de ses variétés prépara la naissance de la pomologie scientifique qui se constitua seulement à partir de la seconde moitié du XIXe siècle. Des jardiniers et des pépiniéristes, mais aussi des amateurs de jardins et de fruits, s'attachèrent à décrire, nommer et classer systématiquement les différentes sortes existantes. Des livres sur la culture des fruits présentèrent les variétés traditionnelles et nouvelles à l'aide de textes et d'illustrations (ill. 1). Des ouvrages spécialisés sur certains types de fruits parurent également, sous le nom de *Pomonas*. Illustrés de magnifiques planches pomologiques, ils connurent un formidable essor et des éditions somptueuses fleurirent à partir du début du XIXe siècle. La *Pomona Britannica* de George Brookshaw, parue en 1812, est la publication anglaise la plus complète sur la question et ses impressions en couleur en font l'une des plus précieuses jamais éditées.

Vie et œuvre de George Brookshaw

George Brookshaw est né en 1751 à Birmingham (Angleterre) et mort en février 1823 à Greenwich près de Londres. Son enfance, sa jeunesse, ses années de formation et sa vie d'adulte nous sont peu connues, et aucun portrait de lui ne nous est parvenu. Brookshaw a probablement reçu une formation artistique de son frère Richard (1736–vers 1804), graveur sur cuivre et spécialiste des techniques d'impression du mezzotinto. Gravant des portraits peints par d'autres artistes, ce dernier s'était fait un nom sur les îles Britanniques mais aussi à Paris où il s'établit également à la fin du XVIIIe siècle, en tant que graveur sur cuivre.

George Brookshaw's work is only ascertainable from 1777, when as a 26-year-old he went to London to work for some 20 years as a cabinetmaker, concentrating his efforts on building very fine, intricately designed pieces of furniture. He was so successful in this trade that he managed to secure the patronage of the English royal family. Documentation of painted pieces of furniture made by Brookshaw is provided by an acknowledgement of receipt by Prince George (1762–1830, from 1820 King George IV). Besides allegorical scenes, these high-quality cabinets, tables and mantelpieces displayed fine illustrations of fruits and floral bouquets. These fruit paintings on wood were an exquisite foretaste of Brookshaw's career change in the last decade of the 18th century.

Brookshaw began to focus more on his exceptional talent as a draughtsman and painter of vegetal motifs on paper. At the same time, he began to explore printing techniques he could use to best effect in reproducing his plant drawings. At the latest by the beginning of the 19th century George Brookshaw had become a valued and admired draughtsman and engraver of fruits and flowers. It was then that he embarked upon the complex and intensive work on his *Pomona Britannica*, which appeared in 1812.

The *Pomona Britannica* of 1812 – a heavenly work

Dedicated to *His Royal Highness, George*, Prince Regent and future King George IV, the *Pomona Britannica* of 1812 looks majestic even before its covers are opened. The pages of the copy in the museum at Greiz measure 580 x 460 mm and are bound between two sturdy book boards covered in contemporary brown leather. Decorative gilt borders are stamped into the leather. The letter *E* is impressed in gold leaf at the centre of both the front and back covers – the initial of Prince George's sister Elizabeth, erstwhile proud owner of this printed edition. The crimson paint on the spine draws the eye to the title of the work, stamped in gilt lettering in Roman capitals: BROOKSHAW'S POMONA BRITANNICA.

George Brookshaw – initiator, author and artist – intended to present the highest-quality fruits being cultivated in the splendid royal gardens at Hampton Court and in the important gardens on the outskirts of London. With this instructive pomological work Brookshaw intended, furthermore, to address country gentlemen in particular and introduce them to the abundance of varieties in an effort to encourage more extensive cultivation.

The *Pomona Britannica* was designed to offer, particularly to noble estate owners and their gardeners, professional aid in distinguishing between the individual types of fruits through "perfect delineation" of the best varieties of the various fruits "with particular descriptions of their characters" by which they distinguish themselves. For, "in planting a new garden, the first grand object is, to consider what are the proper varieties with which the table may be supplied, and the dessert set out with the highest flavored fruit, and from the earliest to the latest period possible". Whoever studied this work would soon have "a garden well planted", of which there were, according to Brookshaw, not many. The author found fault even with some of the most famous gardens in the environs of London. Another purpose of the *Pomona Britannica* was to sort out the "confusion" among the native fruit varieties, to discover their diversity and establish hitherto unknown but excellent varieties.

The way that the *Pomona Britannica* presented the fruits is convincing in every respect. To maintain some overview of the 256 fruit varieties, a practical ordering system had to be found. Fifteen selected species of fruits were presented one after another, each with their own

Namen, sondern er etablierte sich am Ende des 18. Jahrhunderts auch in Paris als Kupferstecher.

Mit Sicherheit lässt sich George Brookshaws Wirken erst mit dem Jahr 1777 erkennen: Als 26-Jähriger ging er nach London, um für die folgenden beinahe 20 Jahre als Möbeltischler tätig zu sein. Er konzentrierte sich auf die Anfertigung von sehr feinem und raffiniert gestaltetem Mobiliar. Durch seine erfolgreiche Etablierung in diesem Handwerk genoss er bald einen solch bedeutenden Ruf, dass ihm auch die Gönnerschaft des englischen Königshauses sicher war. So werden auf einer Empfangsbestätigung des Prinzen George (1762–1830, seit 1820 König George IV.) bemalte Möbel dokumentiert, die Brookshaw angefertigt hatte. Die hochwertigen Schränke, Tische und Kaminsimse waren mit allegorischen Szenen sowie hervorragenden Fruchtdarstellungen und Blumenbouquets bemalt. Diese gemalten Früchte auf Holz waren quasi ein exquisiter Vorgeschmack auf Brookshaws sich verändernde berufliche Aktivitäten in den 90er Jahren des 18. Jahrhunderts. Brookshaw konzentrierte sich nun zunehmend auf sein hervorragendes Talent als Zeichner und Maler von vegetabilen Motiven auf Papier. Zugleich beschäftigte er sich intensiv mit Drucktechniken, die er zur Vervielfältigung seiner gezeichneten Pflanzen effektiv nutzen konnte. Spätestens seit dem Beginn des 19. Jahrhunderts hatte sich George Brookshaw zu einem geschätzten und bewunderten Zeichner und Stecher von Früchten und Blumen profiliert.

Die *Pomona Britannica* von 1812 – ein paradiesisches Früchtewerk

Die *Seiner Königlichen Hoheit George*, dem Prinzregenten und späteren König George IV., gewidmete *Pomona Britannica* von 1812 ist schon im geschlossenen Zustand ein majestätisches Werk. Im Greizer Exemplar messen die Blätter 580 x 460 mm und sind zwischen zwei stabilen, mit zeitgenössischem braunem Leder überzogenen Buchdeckeln gebunden. In das Leder wurden teilweise mit einer Goldauflage versehene Schmuckbordüren eingeprägt. In der Mitte des Buchdeckels befindet sich vorder- wie rückseitig ein ebenfalls in Gold geprägtes *E* – das Signum für die Schwester George IV., Elizabeth, einst stolze Besitzerin dieses Druckexemplars. Mit dem karminroten Farbanstrich eines Buchrückenfeldes wird die Aufmerksamkeit auf den in vergoldeten Antiqua-Großbuchstaben gesetzten Titel des Werkes, BROOKSHAW'S POMONA BRITANNICA, gelenkt.

George Brookshaw – Initiator, Autor und Künstler – beabsichtigte einerseits, die besten und qualitätvollsten Früchte vorzustellen, die in den herrlichen königlichen Gärten von Hampton Court und in den am meisten geschätzten Gärten rund um London angebaut wurden. Andererseits wollte Brookshaw mit seinem pomologisch-lehrenden Beitrag vor allem die reicheren Landbesitzer, die „country gentlemen", ansprechen und durch die Vorstellung der Sortenvielfalt die extensivere Kultivierung von Früchten fördern. Die *Pomona Britannica* sollte vor allem adligen Gartenbesitzern und deren Gärtnern eine professionelle Hilfestellung zur Unterscheidung der einzelnen Fruchtsorten bieten: durch „vollständige Darlegung (der besten Sorten der verschiedenen Früchte) mit besonderer Beschreibung ihrer Charakteristika", anhand derer sie sich unterscheiden. Denn: „beim Bepflanzen eines neuen Gartens ist das Hauptaugenmerk zunächst darauf gerichtet, sich die passenden Obstsorten auszuwählen, mit denen der Tisch gedeckt werden kann, das Dessert mit den geschmackvollsten Früchten gestaltet werden kann und das möglichst von der frühesten bis zur letzten Erntephase". Wer dieses Werk studiere, würde bald einen „gut bepflanzten Garten" besitzen, von denen es nach Brookshaw nicht viele gab; selbst in einigen der berühmtesten Gärten um London herum stellte der Autor Mängel fest. Ein weiterer Nutzen der *Pomona Britannica* sollte die Auflösung des

L'activité de George Brookshaw est seulement attestée avec certitude à partir de l'année 1777 : à 26 ans, il se rend à Londres où il travaille pendant près de vingt ans comme ébéniste, fabriquant des meubles d'une grande finesse, dans un style très raffiné. La renommée que lui vaut ce travail de qualité lui assure aussi la protection de la maison royale d'Angleterre. Ainsi, dans le document de confirmation d'une réception donnée par le prince George (1762–1830, le roi George IV à partir de 1820) figurent des meubles peints, réalisés par Brookshaw. Des scènes allégoriques et d'admirables représentations de fruits et de bouquets de fleurs ornent les armoires, les tables et les dessus de cheminée qu'il peignait avec art. Ses fruits peints sur bois offrent un délicieux avant-goût de la nouvelle activité professionnelle à laquelle il se consacre à partir des années 90 du XVIIIᵉ siècle. En effet, Brookshaw s'adonne de plus en plus à son talent de dessinateur et de peintre de motifs végétaux sur papier. Il s'intéresse aussi activement aux techniques d'impression qui peuvent lui être utiles pour la reproduction de ses dessins de plantes. A partir de la fin du XIXᵉ siècle, l'ébéniste est devenu un dessinateur et graveur de fruits et de fleurs apprécié et admiré.

La Pomona Britannica de 1812, un ouvrage paradisiaque sur les fruits

La *Pomona Britannica* de 1812, dédiée à Son Altesse Royale le prince régent George, devenu plus tard le roi George IV d'Angleterre, est déjà en soi une œuvre royale. Dans l'exemplaire de Greiz, les pages ont un format de 580 x 460 mm et sont reliées à une couverture en cuir brun de l'époque, qui maintient solidement l'ensemble. Des bordures dorées, imprimées sur le cuir, ornent cette couverture. Un E doré, gravé au milieu des première et quatrième de couverture, représente l'initiale de la sœur de George, Elisabeth, fière propriétaire de cet exemplaire imprimé. Sur le dos, une surface rouge carmin met en évidence le titre du livre inscrit en lettres majuscules dorées dans le caractère Antiqua : BROOKSHAW'S POMONA BRITANNICA.

A l'initiative de ce livre, George Brookshaw en était aussi l'auteur et l'illustrateur. Son but avait été, d'une part, de présenter les plus belles et les meilleures qualités de fruits cultivés dans les splendides jardins royaux de Hampton Court ainsi que dans les jardins les plus admirés des environs de Londres. D'autre part, avec cet ouvrage didactique de pomologie, Brookshaw voulait surtout s'adresser aux propriétaires terriens les plus riches – les «country-gentlemen» – et les inciter, par une présentation des multiples variétés existantes, à pratiquer une culture plus extensive. La *Pomona Britannica* visait avant tout à apporter une aide professionnelle aux nobles, propriétaires de jardins, et à leurs jardiniers, afin de leur permettre de distinguer les différentes sortes de fruits grâce à une «présentation complète (des meilleures variétés de chaque fruit), et à une description précise de leurs caractéristiques» distinctives. Car «lorsqu'on plante un nouveau jardin, le premier souci est de choisir les variétés de fruits adéquates, qui orneront la table et permettront de réaliser les desserts les plus savoureux, en profitant si possible de toutes les périodes de récolte, de la plus précoce à la plus tardive». Celui qui étudierait cet ouvrage posséderait bientôt un «jardin bien planté», ce qui, d'après Brookshaw, était une rareté. Car même dans quelques-uns des jardins les plus célèbres de Londres, l'auteur constatait des lacunes. La *Pomona Britannica* devait également permettre de mettre fin à la «confusion» qui régnait parmi les variétés de fruits locales, de découvrir la multiplicité des variétés existantes et de repérer des sortes encore inconnues et pourtant excellentes.

Dans la *Pomona Britannica*, la présentation des fruits est très réussie, à tous points de vue. Pour garder une bonne vue d'ensemble, mal

2

Dosso Dossi
Detail of *Allegory of Hercules (or Sorcery)*, c. 1540–1542
Detail aus *Allegorie des Herkules (oder der Zauberei)*, um 1540–1542
Détail d'*Allégorie avec Hercule (ou Scène de sorcellerie)*, vers 1540–1542
Oil on canvas | Öl auf Leinwand | Huile sur toile, 144 x 143 cm
Florence | Florenz | Florence, Galleria degli Uffizi

3

Pear Harvest in the Orchard, 1768
N. de Launay, copperplate engraving after a drawing by Jacques de Sève

This frontispiece depicts a charming harvest scene: a fruit grower,
standing on a ladder, is most gallantly reaching out to pick the pears
for a woman to gather in her apron; the fruits are also presented to
the viewer in a shallow basket.

Birnenernte im Obstgarten, 1768
N. de Launay, Kupferstich, nach einer Zeichnung von Jacques de Sève

Eine reizende Ernteszene ist auf dem Titelbild dargestellt: äußerst galant
streckt ein auf der Leiter stehender Obstgärtner seinen Arm zum Pflücken
der Birnen aus, die von einer Frau in ihrer Schürze gesammelt und in
einer flachen Korbschale dem Betrachter präsentiert werden.

Récolte de poires dans le verger, 1768
Gravure sur cuivre de N. de Launay, d'après un dessin de Jacques de Sève

Le frontispice représente une ravissante scène de récolte. Un jardinier
monté sur une échelle tend galamment son bras pour cueillir des poires
qu'une femme recueille dans son tablier avant de les présenter au spectateur dans une coupe de fruits peu profonde.

varieties. Under the species heading the respective varieties were first
described and then shown in illustrations. Each numbered illustration
was also featured in the text, so the reader was easily able to seek out
the explanatory text to a specific illustration and vice versa. Starting
with strawberries, the berries or aggregate fruits were introduced: raspberries, currants and gooseberries. There followed a palette of stone
fruits: cherries, plums, apricots, peaches and nectarines. Then pineapples, grapes and melons took the stage. After treating nuts and figs,
the work closed with a presentation of pears and apples, the pomaceous
fruit.

In this sequence, the *Pomona Britannica* also reads like a har-
vester's guide: opening with the early ripeners in June, strawberries,
the work closes with the latecomers, apples, some varieties of which
were picked at the very end of the harvesting season (ill. 3). Brookshaw
designed the 90 plates in the *Pomona Britannica* with care. He could
have consigned a plate to each variety, as numerous other contemporary work about fruits had done. But then, in order to accommodate the
same number of varieties, printing costs would have risen so drastically
that not even the most liberal of patrons would have obliged. To remain
within the given financial constraints, Brookshaw might also have
reduced the number of illustrated fruit varieties. But since his main
purpose was to publish the largest-possible selection of varieties,
displaying several fruits on each plate ultimately offered him the most
effective use of the available pictorial space.

The illustrations in the *Pomona Britannica* seem to glow in a sweet
and soft light, which is mainly due to the printing technique used,
aquatint. The fruits are rarely presented on a white background; often
they are set against various shades of contrasting browns. Because
Brookshaw wanted to depict the fruit varieties as true-to-life as possible,
for the sake of easy recognition, he had to take their natural sizes into
account as well. Accordingly, a single pineapple fills the whole picture field of a plate, or a single bunch of grapes or melon gourd. The
melons, surrounded by their trailing vines, flowers and leaves, are won-
derfully positioned on their rootstocks. The smaller fruits, however, are
arranged in groups on the individual plates: at least two varieties each
per illustration, such as for the raspberries, to a maximum of 17 varieties, such as for the gooseberries, mostly displayed in threes or fours.
Thus he presented very attractive arrangements inviting the viewer to
linger over plump strawberries and gooseberries, velvety purple plums,
succulent pale-green pears, delicately structured pineapples and glowing red-and-yellow peaches. By contrast, most of the apples, which
without their leafy bowers seem virtually naked, are composed within
a quite rigid order.

Brookshaw's carefully thought out grouping of the fruits must have
been warmly received, for it provided a more effective way to compare
the individual varieties of a species of fruit. The limited space available
to each fruit variety meant that each reproduction had to be reduced to
the essentials while still taking into account the defining morphological
characteristics of the variety. This was crucial for precise identification
and practical use of the varieties in horticulture, and is why the fruits
were not always depicted by themselves but frequently together with
characteristic sections of the plant, such as leaves and blossoms (ill. 4).
Maximum precision was sought in representing the vegetal parts, the
sizes, shapes, textures and colours, in order to facilitate recognition and
distinction between the individual varieties. In reflecting the individual
characteristics of the fruit varieties, appropriate selection and skilful
use of the artistic techniques played an enormous role as well.

Some varieties among the impressive number of fruit illustrations
are hardly distinguishable from one another. Even the leaves and blos-

„Durcheinanders" unter den einheimischen Fruchtsorten sein, das Entdecken der Sortenvielfalt und die Etablierung noch unbekannter, aber exzellenter Sorten.

Die Präsentation der Früchte gelingt in der *Pomona Britannica* in jeder Hinsicht überzeugend. Um bei der großen Anzahl von 256 Fruchtsorten den Überblick zu garantieren, musste ein praktisches Ordnungsschema gefunden werden. Nacheinander werden 15 ausgewählte Fruchtarten mit ihren jeweiligen Sorten vorgestellt, wobei unter der Überschrift einer Fruchtart zunächst die zugehörigen Sorten beschrieben und anschließend auf Abbildungen präsentiert werden. Da jede Abbildungsnummer auch als kleine Überschrift im Text erscheint, kann der Leser sich gezielt den ergänzenden Text zur jeweiligen Abbildung und umgekehrt heraussuchen. Beginnend mit den Erdbeeren werden zunächst die Beeren- bzw. Sammelfrüchte vorgestellt: Himbeeren, Johannisbeeren und Stachelbeeren. Es folgt die breite Palette des sogenannten Steinobstes: Kirschen, Pflaumen, Aprikosen, Pfirsiche und Nektarinen, dann dominieren Ananas, Weintrauben und Melonen. Nachdem Nüsse und Feigen abgehandelt sind, wird das Werk mit der Vorstellung der Birnen und Äpfel, dem Kernobst, abgeschlossen. In dieser Fruchtreihenfolge liest sich die *Pomona Britannica* auch wie ein Erntebuch: Beginnend mit den zuerst reifenden Erdbeeren ab Juni bis zu den Äpfeln, die das baldige Ende der Erntesaison einläuten und von denen einige Sorten die zuletzt zu pflückenden Früchte sind (Abb. 3)

Die Gestaltung der 90 Tafeln in der *Pomona Britannica* hat Brookshaw wohl überlegt. Einerseits hätte er jeder Sorte eine eigene Tafel zugestehen können, wie es zahlreiche Beispiele in zeitgenössischen Früchtewerken belegen. Bei gleich bleibender Sortenzahl wären allerdings die Kosten für den Druck so enorm angestiegen, dass selbst der freizügigste Mäzen die Flucht ergriffen hätte. Um den finanziellen Rahmen nicht zu überschreiten, hätte Brookshaw andererseits die Anzahl der abzubildenden Fruchtsorten wesentlich reduzieren können. Doch weil er sein Hauptaugenmerk gerade auf die Veröffentlichung einer möglichst großen Sortenzahl legte, bot sich für ihn in der Präsentation von mehreren Früchten auf einer Tafel schließlich eine effektive Nutzung der Bildflächen.

Die Abbildungen in der *Pomona Britannica* strahlen eine liebliche und weiche Atmosphäre aus, was vor allem aus der angewandten Drucktechnik der Aquatinta resultiert. Die Früchte werden selten vor einem weiß belassenen Bildhintergrund präsentiert; oftmals sind sie von verschiedenen Brauntönen kontrastierend hinterfangen. Da Brookshaw die Fruchtsorten für deren Wiedererkennung möglichst naturgetreu abbilden wollte, musste er unter anderem ihre natürliche Größe berücksichtigen. Entsprechend ist bei den Ananasfrüchten, Weintrauben und Melonen nur eine, das gesamte Bildformat ausfüllende Sorte pro Tafel dargestellt. Die von Ranken, Blüten und Blättern umgebenen Melonen sind wunderbar auf einer Unterlage positioniert. Die kleineren Früchte wurden hingegen auf den einzelnen Tafeln in Gruppen arrangiert: Von mindestens zwei Sorten je Abbildung wie zum Beispiel bei den Himbeeren bis zu maximal 17 Sorten wie zum Beispiel bei den Stachelbeeren sind vor allem Früchtetrios und -quartetts präsent. Dabei gelangen Brookshaw sehr ansprechende, zum Verweilen einladende Arrangements von großen Erdbeeren und Stachelbeeren, von faszinierend violetten Pflaumen, saftig gelbgrünen Birnen, filigran strukturierten Ananasfrüchten und von leuchtend gelb-roten Pfirsichen. Hingegen sind die meisten Äpfel, die ohne das schmückende Beiwerk des Blattgrüns beinahe entblößt wirken, nach einem etwas starr anmutenden Kompositionsschema angeordnet.

Brookshaws wohl überlegtes Gruppieren der Früchte wurde sehr begrüßt, da auf diese Weise die einzelnen Sorten einer Fruchtart noch ef-

gré les 256 variétés de fruits décrits, il a fallu trouver un ordre de classement pratique. 15 espèces de fruits, soigneusement choisies, sont présentées les unes après les autres. Pour chacune, l'auteur donne une description de ses diverses variétés, accompagnées d'illustrations. Chaque numéro d'illustration correspond dans le texte à un sous-titre suivi d'une description, de sorte que le lecteur peut directement se reporter au texte d'une illustration ou inversement, à l'illustration correspondant à un texte. Le livre commence par les baies : fraises, framboises, groseilles et groseilles à maquereau. Leur succède toute une gamme de fruits à noyau : cerises, prunes, abricots, pêches et nectarines. Puis viennent l'ananas, les raisins et les melons, qui occupent une position dominante. Après avoir traité les noix et les figues, l'ouvrage se termine avec les fruits à pépins : poires et pommes. Dans cet ordre, la *Pomona Britannica* se lit aussi comme un livre des récoltes. Commençant par la fraise, qui se cueille en premier, à partir du mois de juin, il se termine par les pommes qui annoncent la fin des récoltes et dont certaines variétés se ramassent très tard (ill. 3).

La conception des 90 planches de la *Pomona Britannica* a été mûrement réfléchie. Brookshaw aurait pu, comme de nombreux auteurs d'ouvrages de fruits à l'époque, consacrer une planche à chaque sorte. Mais les coûts d'impression auraient été si considérables que même le mécène le plus généreux aurait pris la fuite. Pour rester dans des limites financières raisonnables, Brookshaw aurait pu considérablement réduire le nombre de fruits à représenter. Mais comme il lui importait par-dessus tout de publier le plus grand nombre possible de variétés, il résolut la question en reproduisant plusieurs fruits par planche.

Les illustrations de la *Pomona Britannica* baignent dans une atmosphère douce et agréable, due surtout à la technique d'impression utilisée, l'aquatinte. Les fruits sont rarement représentés sur fond blanc mais sur des tons bruns contrastés. Voulant rendre les fruits clairement reconnaissables, Brookshaw s'était efforcé de les reproduire aussi fidèlement que possible, notamment en ce qui concerne leur taille. C'est pourquoi chaque variété d'ananas, de raisin et de melon occupe une planche entière. Les melons, entourés de leurs vrilles, fleurs et feuilles ressortent admirablement sur le fond qui leur a été donné. Les fruits plus petits, en revanche, sont regroupés dans les différentes planches, au minimum par deux comme les framboises, au maximum par 17 comme les groseilles à maquereau, mais en général par trois ou quatre. Brookshaw a ainsi réalisé des arrangements très plaisants et très réussis de grandes fraises et de groseilles à maquereau, de fascinantes prunes violettes, de poires juteuses vert-jaunes, d'ananas parcourus de filigranes et de pêches à la peau jaune-rouge brillante, donnant au lecteur l'envie de s'attarder. En revanche, la plupart des pommes, qui paraîtraient presque nues sans leurs ornements de feuilles vertes, sont disposées selon un modèle de composition assez rigide.

Ces groupements de fruits, très étudiés, ont été beaucoup appréciés, car ils permettaient de mieux comparer encore les différentes variétés d'une même espèce. En raison du peu de place qui pouvait être consacré à chaque sorte de fruit, il fallait, dans la représentation, aller à l'essentiel, tout en respectant les principales caractéristiques morphologiques de chaque sorte : condition indispensable pour la détermination exacte des variétés et leur culture concrète dans les vergers (ill. 4). C'est pourquoi les illustrations ne se limitent pas à la représentation des seuls fruits mais s'efforcent aussi de donner un aperçu des éléments caractéristiques de la plante porteuse, comme les feuilles et les fleurs. L'auteur a donc cherché à reproduire avec autant d'exactitude que possible les différentes parties de la plante, dans le respect des dimensions, des formes, des matières et des couleurs. Le choix et la maîtrise des techniques artistiques adéquates a également joué un rôle considérable

soms are sometimes so bewilderingly similar that they would confuse anyone trying to compare them. In order for readers to derive the full benefit of the available pomological knowledge, each illustration was preceded by a description of the individual varieties depicted. The associated text outlines characteristics that cannot be illustrated, such as the flavour of the pulp and preferred uses of the fruits.

An index fills the last pages of the work, allowing quick reference or targeted searches from among all the illustrated varieties: from A as in "Antwerp White Raspberry" to W as in "Winter Swan's Egg Pear". Reading the descriptions and looking at the illustrations, a modern user will surely experience the same delight and the same overwhelming sense of nature's abundance as Brookshaw's contemporaries. But a parting glance at the list of varieties is a sobering reminder of the drastic reduction in the number of cultivars over the course of almost two centuries, mostly for economic reasons. One more excuse to while in Brookshaw's lost paradise of fruits.

The legacy of the *Pomona Britannica*

After the striking success of the *Pomona Britannica*, Brookshaw continued to work along the same lines. Just five years after the appearance of the major work, he released a smaller edition on the same subject in quarto format (335 x 270 mm). It bore the same title and was printed in London by Bensley & Son. Sixty illustration plates depicted 174 varieties of fruits, each set on a blank white background. They are pleasingly composed aquatint colour prints in the stipple manner, subsequently painted in watercolour and opaque white. The artistic design and high print quality of this volume are very effective; no less so its transmission of pomological information. Some text passages and picture motifs were taken from its forerunner, nevertheless this smaller work could not achieve quite the same repute as the edition from 1812.

Not that it was Brookshaw's intention to publish a competitor to the large *Pomona Britannica*. This less expensive variant from 1817 addressed growers of more modest circumstances, with tighter purses, smaller pieces of land, and no greenhouses. Thus Brookshaw demonstrated his ability as an author and an illustrator. But he was equally proficient as an instructor – in the area of fruit and flower painting. In 1816 the *New Treatise on Flower Painting* appeared, followed by its supplement in 1817. In the subtitle to his first instructions on flower painting he held out the prospect of "every Lady her own drawing master." Brookshaw's *Groups of Fruits* appeared in 1817 in folio (360 x 260 mm) in London, printed by Augustus Applegath & Henry Mitton; its second edition is dated 1819. This text introduced the basic artistic techniques for drawing and painting fruits. In the same year that the *Groups of Fruits* appeared, other instruction manuals on drawing flowers and birds were released: *Groups of Flowers* and *Six Birds*, their second editions likewise appearing two years later.

The best English fruit varieties were featured one more time in Brookshaw's *Horticultural Repository*, which laid out verbally and visually the essential observations for a successful fruit plantation. The printed work in octavo format appeared posthumously in 1823. Its foreword is unsigned, written by a person who had known Brookshaw well, having kept his company through the last years of his life. He characterized his friend as an "able artist, and observing horticulturist", one of those "persons of genius and of talent who labour for the pleasures and conveniences of their species; yet, who live almost unknown, and sink into the tomb unheard of and undistinguished."

fektiver miteinander verglichen werden konnten. Entsprechend der geringen, jeder Fruchtsorte zugestandenen Bildteilfläche musste die Wiedergabe der einzelnen Sorten unter Berücksichtigung der jeweils wichtigen morphologischen Kennzeichen jeder Sorte auf das Wesentliche reduziert werden. Dies war für eine exakte Bestimmung und für die Nutzung der Sorten im praktischen Obstbau unabdingbar (Abb. 4). Daher sind oftmals nicht nur die Früchte, sondern auch charakteristische Ausschnitte der jeweils Frucht tragenden Pflanze wie Blätter und Blüten dargestellt. Um eine Erfolg versprechende Wiedererkennung und Unterscheidung der einzelnen Sorten zu garantieren, wurde eine möglichst exakte Wiedergabe der vegetabilen Pflanzenteile in Größe, Form, Materialität und Farbe angestrebt. Um den Fruchtsorten ihr jeweils charakteristisches Aussehen zu geben, spielte auch die treffliche Auswahl und der gekonnte Umgang mit den künstlerischen Techniken eine enorme Rolle. Bei der beeindruckenden Anzahl abgebildeter Früchte sind einige Sorten dabei, die sich nur minimal voneinander unterscheiden. Selbst die Blätter und Blüten sind manchmal so verblüffend ähnlich, dass sie den Betrachter beim Vergleichen der Sorten verwirren. Um den Gewinn an pomologischem Wissen und die bildliche Präsenz der Fruchtsorten in vollen Zügen genießen zu können, sind die Abbildungen durch jeweils vorangestellte Beschreibungen der einzelnen Sorten ergänzt worden. In den zugehörigen Texten sind nicht darstellbare Fruchtmerkmale wie zum Beispiel der Geschmack des Fruchtfleisches und bevorzugte Verwendungsmöglichkeiten der Früchte beschrieben.

Auf den letzten Seiten des Werkes befindet sich ein Register, das das schnelle und gezielte Aufsuchen aller dargestellten Fruchtsorten ermöglicht: von A wie „Antwerp White Raspberry" (Weiße Antwerpener Himbeere) bis W wie „Winter Swan's Egg Pear" (Schwanenei-Birne). Beim Lesen der Fruchtbeschreibungen und vor allem beim Ansehen der Abbildungen kann der heutige Betrachter sicherlich ein ähnliches Entzücken und eine ähnliche Überwältigung verspüren wie Brookshaws Zeitgenossen. Doch spätestens ein nüchterner Blick auf die Sortenliste kann auch eine melancholische Stimmung auslösen. Im Laufe der letzten beinahe zwei Jahrhunderte wurde die Sortenvielfalt vor allem aus wirtschaftlichen Gründen drastisch reduziert. Ein Grund mehr, in Brookshaws untergegangenem Paradies der Früchte zu verweilen.

Die Wirkungsgeschichte der *Pomona Britannica*

Nach dem herausragenden Erfolg der *Pomona Britannica* arbeitete Brookshaw in dieser Richtung weiter und bereits fünf Jahre nach dem Erscheinen der *Pomona Britannica* gab er unter demselben Titel ein kleineres Früchtebuch im Quarto-Format (335 x 270 mm) heraus, das in London bei Bensley & Sohn gedruckt wurde. Brookshaw stellte auf 60 Abbildungstafeln 174 Fruchtsorten vor einem jeweils weiß belassenen Hintergrund dar. Er brillierte mit farbig gedruckten Aquatinten, die mit Punktiermanier harmonisch kombiniert und nachträglich mit Wasserfarben und Deckweiß koloriert sind. Unzweifelhaft ist bei diesem Früchtewerk die künstlerische Gestaltung und Druckqualität sehr hochwertig, so wie auch die Vermittlung pomologischen Wissens hervorragend gelang. Teilweise wurden Textpassagen und Bildmotive aus dem Vorgängerwerk übernommen. Die Wirkung der Ausgabe von 1812 konnte dieses kleinere Früchtewerk jedoch nicht ganz erzielen. Es war von Brookshaw wohl auch nicht beabsichtigt, eine mit der großen *Pomona Britannica* konkurrierende Druckausgabe herauszugeben. Vielmehr wollte er mit dieser preisgünstigeren Variante von 1817 wohl die bescheidener lebenden Gärtner mit kleineren Grundstücken, ohne Gewächshäuser und mit schmaleren Geldbeuteln ansprechen.

Brookshaw bewies nicht nur seine Fähigkeiten als Autor und Künstler, sondern ebenso als Lehrender – sowohl auf dem Gebiet der Frucht-

dans cette tentative de donner à chaque variété son apparence caractéristique. Parmi la quantité considérable de fruits représentés, il existe
toutefois quelques sortes d'apparence très semblable. La ressemblance
va parfois jusqu'aux feuilles et aux fleurs. Mais pour dispenser le maximum de connaissances pomologiques et permettre au lecteur de tirer
le meilleur parti des reproductions, celles-ci sont toutes précédées
d'une description écrite de la variété correspondante dont elle énumère
les caractéristiques importantes – telles que le goût ou les meilleures
manières de les utiliser – qui ne peuvent pas se représenter dans une
image.

Les dernières pages de l'ouvrage comportent un index qui permet
de retrouver facilement les sortes de fruits recherchées par le lecteur :
de A comme « Antwerp White Raspberry » (framboise blanche d'Anvers
à gros fruit) jusqu'à W comme « Winter Swan's Egg Pear » (poire d'hiver
œuf de cygne). A la lecture des descriptions de fruits, et surtout à la vue
des illustrations, le lecteur moderne éprouvera sans doute un ravissement et une émotion semblables à ceux que pouvaient ressentir les contemporains de Brookshaw. Mais la longue liste des variétés traitées peut
laisser rêveur. En près de deux siècles, cette étonnante diversité a, pour
des raisons essentiellement économiques, terriblement diminué. Une
raison de plus pour s'attarder un moment dans ce paradis perdu des
fruits de Brookshaw.

L'impact de la *Pomona Britannica*

Après l'extraordinaire succès de la *Pomona Britannica*, Brookshaw
poursuit ses travaux dans la même direction, et cinq ans après la parution de sa *Pomona Britannica*, il publie déjà, sous le même titre, un
petit fascicule au format in-quarto (335 x 270 mm), imprimé à Londres
chez Bensley & Fils. Il contient 174 sortes de fruits représentées sur 60
planches à fond blanc. Les admirables reproductions en couleur allient
harmonieusement deux techniques d'impression : l'aquatinte et la
gravure en pointillé, avant d'être coloriées à l'aquarelle et à la gouache
blanche. D'une conception artistique et d'une qualité d'impression exceptionnelles, cet ouvrage sur les fruits est également remarquable par
les connaissances pomologiques qu'il communique. Certains passages
et certaines illustrations ont été repris de l'ouvrage précédent. Mais cet
ouvrage plus petit n'a cependant pas pu prétendre au succès de l'édition
de 1812. Brookshaw ne semblait pas non plus avoir eu l'intention de ri-
valiser avec son ouvrage précédent. Mais sans doute a-t-il voulu, avec
cette version moins coûteuse de 1817, s'adresser à un public de jardiniers plus modestes, travaillant sur des surfaces plus petites, sans serres
et sans grands moyens.

Dans ses ouvrages, Brookshaw a fait la preuve de ses talents d'auteur
et d'artiste, mais aussi d'enseignant – en peinture de fruits et de fleurs.
En 1816 paraît son *New Treatise on Flower Painting*, suivi d'un supplé-
ment en 1817. Le sous-titre de son premier manuel de peinture de fleurs
proclame : « chaque dame, son propre professeur de peinture ». En 1817
paraît à Londres son *Groups of Fruits*, réédité en format in-folio (360 x
260 mm) en 1819 et imprimé par Augustus Applegath & Henry Mitton.
Dans ce manuel à la fois technique et artistique, l'auteur transmet les
connaissances de base nécessaires pour dessiner et colorier des fruits.
Il fait également paraître parallèlement en 1817, et rééditer en 1819, des
manuels de dessin de fleurs et d'oiseaux : *Groups of Flowers* et *Six
Birds*. Dans son *Horticultural Repository*, Brookshaw présente encore
une fois en mots et en images les meilleures sortes de fruits anglaises
avec d'importantes observations pour bien les cultiver. L'ouvrage imprimé au format in-octavo parut après sa mort, en 1823. L'avant-propos
est rédigé par un auteur inconnu, qui avait accompagné Brookshaw du-
rant les derniers mois de sa vie et qui le décrit de la manière suivante :

4

Design for Garden Grounds with a large Orchard, 1799
Unknown artist, copperplate engraving from J.V. Sickler's periodical
Der teutsche Obstgärtner

In Sickler's suggested layout for a garden – from north to south: summer
house, flower beds, orchard, landscape park – the largest area, which is
assigned to the orchard, is efficiently planted with ranks of bushes and
trees arranged by growth height; these rigid plantation rows are relaxed
by the curving main pathways.

Entwurf einer Gartenanlage mit großem Obstgarten, 1799
Unbekannter Künstler, Kupferstich aus J.V. Sicklers Zeitschrift
Der teutsche Obstgärtner

In Sicklers Vorschlag für eine Gartenanlage – von Nord nach Süd:
Gartenhaus, Blumengarten, Obstgarten, Landschaftspark – wird die
dem Obstgarten zugestandene größte Fläche optimal genutzt durch
eine gestaffelte Anordnung der Sträucher und Bäume je nach Wuchs-
höhe, wobei die Reihenpflanzungen durch geschwungene Hauptwege
aufgelockert sind.

Plan d'un jardin avec grand verger, 1799
Artiste inconnu, gravure sur cuivre de la revue *Der teutsche Obstgärtner*
de J.V. Sickler

Dans la proposition de Sickler pour un aménagement de jardin – du nord
au sud : maison de jardin, jardin de fleurs, verger, parc paysager. La surface consacrée au verger est exploitée au maximum grâce à une disposition
étagée des buissons et des arbres en fonction de leur hauteur, la monoto-
nie des rangées étant déjouée par le dessin sinueux des allées principales.

5

Pomona Britannica, Plate | Tafel | Planche LXXXIX
Phoenix Apple · Norman's Beauty
Kaiser Alexander · Schöner aus Norfolk
Empereur Alexandre · Beauty de Normandie

The printing techniques used for the *Pomona Britannica* – a carefully devised system

The naturalness of Brookshaw's fruit illustrations is as impressive as their aesthetic appeal. The plates in the *Pomona Britannica* are aquatints harmoniously combined with stippling and copperplate engraving (ill. 5). The motifs were printed on the paper generally using only two inks, never more than three, but occasionally with only one, and subsequently painted completely by hand in watercolour and opaque white.

It is clear that Brookshaw could not carry out this complex procedure single-handedly. Most of the prints have a small plaque along their lower edge indicating, besides the plate number and year of completion, the information: "Painted & Published as the Act directs by the Author G. Brookshaw." Hence Brookshaw directed and supervised the whole printing process. It may be assumed that, like many artists before and after him, he first prepared watercolours or at least drawings of the fruits to serve as models for his collaborators during and following the printing process. Brookshaw certainly engraved some of the copperplates himself but without the assistance of other engravers and watercolourists he would not have managed to complete the project in the given period of time. Despite the many busy hands involved, this gigantic project required almost a decade to be completed. The prints are dated March 1804–1812. Of these years, 1806 and 1807 were the most fruitful – in the full sense of the word – with 15 and 25 aquatints prepared, respectively. Unfortunately, only one plate, Plate XLVIII: "Royal Muscadine Grape", identifies the engraver: H. Merke. Who he was remains as obscure as the identities of all the other able collaborators on this project, who implemented Brookshaw's artistic designs with great subtlety and conversant use of the printing and painting methods.

As sumptuous as the fruit prints appear, as arduous was their making in T. Bensley's printing workshop in London. Copper plates of different sizes were used: the dimensions of the 13 smaller plates are about 410 x 310 mm. The majority of the larger plates measured about 450 x 350 mm or more. The worked surface is about the same on all the copper plates. The engravers achieved this uniformity by working over the entire surface of the smaller plates, while leaving wider unworked margins around the larger ones. In preparing a plate for printing, first outlines of the image from Brookshaw's model were drawn on a trimmed blank copper plate. Then a thin layer of acid-resistant varnish was spread over the areas of the plate requiring work only at a later stage, if at all. Aquatint was used for illustration plates with a dark background. The engravers also used this etching procedure for the fruits, leaves, blossoms, stalks and branch sections.

For the background, tiny grains of dust were strewn on the copper plate and fixed so that in subsequent prolonged or multiple baths the acid could bite into the exposed metal surface in the proportionately larger areas between the particles. All the resulting minute pits in the metal could retain enough printer's ink to give a richer, more solid tone to the background on the final paper print. For the fruit motifs, on the other hand, dust particles of different grain sizes were scattered in various densities over the copper plate and the etching was performed variously in order to reproduce the respective surface structures of the fruits as characteristically as possible. That is also how the three-dimensional effect of the fruits was achieved. To augment further the realistic appearance particularly of the fruits, Brookshaw and his collaborators employed the stipple method. Using the sharp or blunt spikes of a roulette, they could work over chosen areas of the plate surface. The resulting regular rows of dots or dashes become clearly visible under a

wie auch der Blumenmalerei. Im Jahre 1816 erschien *New Treatise on Flower Painting*, 1817 das zugehörige Supplement. Mit seiner ersten Anleitung zum Blumenmalen garantierte er laut Untertitel „every Lady her own drawing master". Im Jahre 1817 und in einer zweiten Auflage von 1819 erschien im Folio-Format (360 x 260 mm) Brookshaws *Groups of Fruits* in London, gedruckt von Augustus Applegath & Henry Mitton. In dieser künstlerisch-technischen Anleitung vermittelt er das zum Zeichnen und Kolorieren von Früchten erforderliche Grundwissen. Neben den *Groups of Fruits* erschienen ebenfalls 1817 und in zweiter Auflage 1819 Anleitungsbücher zum Zeichnen von Blumen und Vögeln: *Groups of Flowers* und *Six Birds*. Im *Horticultural Repository* stellte Brookshaw nochmals die besten englischen Fruchtsorten in Wort und Bild vor und vermittelte wesentliche Beobachtungen, die für eine erfolgreiche Kultivierung der Früchte notwendig sind. Das Druckwerk im Oktav-Format erschien im Jahre 1823 postum. Das Vorwort zu diesem Werk schrieb ein unbekannter Autor, der Brookshaw während dessen letzten Lebensmonaten begleitete und ihn wie folgt charakterisierte: George Brookshaw war ein „begabter Künstler und aufmerksamer Gartenbaufachmann", einer von jenen „Genies und Talenten, die für das Vergnügen und die Bequemlichkeit anderer arbeiteten; doch er lebte beinahe unbekannt und nicht einmal am Grabe wurde ihm eine gebührende Ehre zuteil."

Die Drucktechnik der *Pomona Britannica* – ein ausgetüfteltes System

Die naturgetreue und zugleich ästhetische Wirkung von Brookshaws Fruchtdarstellungen ist beeindruckend. Bei den Bildtafeln in der *Pomona Britannica* handelt es sich um Aquatinten in harmonischer Verbindung mit Punktiermanier und partiellem Kupferstich (Abb. 5). Nur mit durchschnittlich zwei, höchstens drei Druckfarben, manchmal aber nur mit einer Farbe wurden die Motive von der Kupferplatte auf Papier gedruckt und anschließend mit Wasserfarben und Deckweiß umfassend koloriert.

Es ist verständlich, dass dieser komplexe Arbeitsprozess von Brookshaw nicht allein bewältigt werden konnte. Auf den meisten Drucken befindet sich am unteren Rand ein kleines mitgedrucktes Täfelchen, auf dem nicht nur die Nummerierung der Bildtafel und deren Entstehungsjahr angegebenen sind, sondern ebenso der Hinweis: „Painted & Published as the Act directs by the Author G. Brookshaw." Dementsprechend lenkte und überwachte Brookshaw den gesamten Entstehungsprozess der Drucke. Es kann angenommen werden, dass er wie viele Künstler vor und nach ihm zunächst Aquarelle oder zumindest Zeichnungen der Früchte anfertigte, die allen Mitarbeitern als Vorlagen während und nach dem Druckprozess dienten. Mit Sicherheit hat Brookshaw einige Kupferplatten selbst bearbeitet, aber ohne die Mithilfe weiterer Stecher und Koloristen hätte er das Projekt in diesem Zeitraum wohl nicht bewältigen können. Trotz der vielen fleißigen Hände wurden für die Umsetzung dieses gigantischen Projekts beinahe zehn Jahre benötigt. Die Drucke sind von März 1804 bis 1812 datiert. Davon waren die Jahre 1806 und 1807 wohl im wahrsten Sinne des Wortes die Fruchtbarsten mit je 15 bzw. 25 angefertigten Aquatinten. Leider befindet sich nur auf einer Bildtafel, Plate XLVIII: „Royal Muscadine Grape", der Name eines Stechers: H. Merke. Wer er war, bleibt ebenso im Unklaren wie sämtliche weiteren Beteiligten an diesem Projekt, die mit großem Einfühlungsvermögen und absolut sicherem Umgang mit den Drucktechniken und der Kolorierung Brookshaws künstlerische Vorstellungen umsetzten.

So genussvoll wie die Fruchtsorten im Druck wirken, so mühevoll war der Entstehungsprozess der Drucke in der Werkstatt von T. Bensley

George Brookshaw était un « artiste talentueux et un horticulteur observateur », un de ces « génies et talents, qui œuvrent pour le plaisir et le bien-être de leurs semblables. Mais il resta quasiment un inconnu. Même dans la tombe, il ne reçut pas les honneurs qui lui étaient dus. »

La technique d'impression de la *Pomona Britannica* – un système très étudié

La fidélité à la nature et l'effet esthétique des représentations de fruits de Brookshaw laissent admiratifs. Dans la *Pomona Britannica*, les planches sont réalisées à l'aquatinte, harmonieusement complétée par la technique du pointillé et parfois, par la gravure sur cuivre (ill. 5). Les motifs de la planche de cuivre étaient généralement imprimés sur le papier en seulement deux couleurs, trois au maximum et parfois une seule, puis abondamment colorés à l'aquarelle et à la gouache blanche.

Il est clair que Brookshaw ne pouvait réaliser à lui seul ce processus d'impression complexe. Sur la plupart des planches, un petit écriteau imprimé dans le bord inférieur indique non seulement le numéro de la planche et de l'année de création mais aussi cette phrase : « Painted & Published as the Act directs by the Author G. Brookshaw. » Brookshaw dirigeait et surveillait donc du début à la fin l'ensemble du processus de réalisation. On peut supposer qu'il réalisait dans un premier temps, comme beaucoup d'artistes avant et après lui, des aquarelles, ou au moins des dessins de fruits, qui servaient de modèle à tous ses collaborateurs pendant et après le processus d'impression. Il est certain aussi que Brookshaw confectionnait lui-même certaines plaques d'impression, mais il n'aurait sans doute pas pu mener à bien son projet dans le même temps sans la collaboration d'autres graveurs et coloristes. Malgré le nombre de mains qui y participèrent activement, il fallut près de dix ans pour réaliser ce gigantesque projet. Les impressions sont datées de mars 1804 à 1812. Les années 1806 et 1807 semblent avoir été les plus fécondes, avec la réalisation de respectivement 15 et 25 aquatintes. Malheureusement, on ne trouve que sur une seule planche (pl. XLVIII, « Royal Muscadine Grape ») le nom d'un graveur, H. Merke. On ne sait rien d'autre à son sujet, ni au sujet des autres collaborateurs au projet, qui ont su avec une grande sensibilité et une parfaite maîtrise des techniques d'impression et de coloration, traduire sur papier les idées artistiques de Brookshaw.

Le plaisir que l'on a à contempler les fruits représentés n'a d'égal que les efforts exigés par le processus d'impression dans l'atelier de T. Bensley à Londres. On utilisait des plaques de cuivre de différentes tailles. Les 13 plus petites mesuraient environ 410 x 310 mm, les plus grandes, de loin les plus nombreuses, environ 450 x 350 mm ou davantage. Mais la surface travaillée sur chaque planche est à peu près la même. Cet ajustement est l'œuvre des graveurs, qui ont su travailler les plaques plus petites sur toute leur surface, jusqu'au bord, et laisser une marge plus large tout autour des plaques plus grandes. Une plaque était réalisée de la manière suivante : les contours des motifs étaient d'abord dessinés d'après le modèle fourni par Brookshaw, sur une plaque de cuivre vierge, coupée aux bonnes dimensions. Puis une fine couche de vernis, résistant aux acides, était appliquée sur toutes les parties de la plaque qui ne devaient être travaillées qu'ultérieurement ou pas du tout. Les planches à fond sombre étaient traitées à l'aquatinte, procédé de gravure à l'eau-forte que les graveurs utilisèrent également pour la réalisation des fruits, des feuilles, des fleurs, des tiges et des morceaux de branches. Pour le fond, on fixait sur la plaque une poudre faite de grains minuscules, de manière à ce que pendant les bains d'acide prolongés ou répétés auxquels était soumise la plaque, les surfaces non vernies du métal fussent gravées en profondeur. Les minuscules sillons ainsi creusés dans le métal pouvaient retenir suffisamment de couleur pour

magnifying glass. Finally, employing the method of line engraving, the engraver could also cut individual burrs out of the metal using a burin. These printed lines served to accentuate the veins on leaves or as contours or hachures for shading and cast shadows. The decoratively framed inscription plate often appearing at the lower edge was also produced by this printing technique. The plates displaying pineapples, grapes and melons indicate Brookshaw's involvement at the lower blank margin of the copper plate, between the plate edge and the aquatint area. Since in these cases only one fruit was depicted per plate, there was room left to engrave the name of the relevant variety.

Once the image had been transferred onto the copper plate, the remaining protective layer was removed and a single-colour test print was made. On the basis of this proof Brookshaw could check the quality of the work thus far and the overall effect of the illustration. The heavy pressure placed on the copper plate also softened the freshly cut image contours. Then the copper plate and the paper, bearing the watermark J. WHATMAN, were prepared for the first printing. A mixture of linseed oil and varnish gave the inks a viscous consistency to prevent them from smudging later on the page. A bundle of fabric, or mull wrapped around a fingertip, was used to dab up to three different inks onto predesignated areas of the motif. Then the printer wiped the plate surface clean so that only the troughs still carried the ink.

The shade of brown used for the background and captions was frequently also used for fruits, flowers, stalks and occasionally even for leaves, where they were not printed in green. Bright red fruits were printed not in red, as one might expect, but in a reddish brown. How could this possibly bring about such a vivid result? Depending on the depths of the tiny etched recesses and their proximity to one another, differing amounts of ink were retained, so the amount of ink deposited on the paper varied correspondingly along with the resulting hue that could be achieved. The result was that one ink alone could produce a range of subtle shades on the page. Afterwards watercolour artists, who were frequently female, painstakingly applied various watercolours using a paintbrush. Sometimes the colours were mixed with opaque white. At this stage of the work, too, relatively few colours were needed. A single pigment applied on top of a given ink would have various results, depending on the intensity of the inked area. This palette of colours could be extended by the degree of dilution of the applied paint. All in all, printing with a limited number of inks and relatively few watercolours is a matter of extreme skill, if the aim is to produce such delightfully brilliant lustre and glowing, fiery tints.

There can be no doubt that producing the *Pomona Britannica* demanded of Brookshaw, in particular, an enormous about of concentration, work, and coordination in order to bring the multifarious tasks to a successful conclusion after all the years of labour. During this period, minor hitches and oversights did arise, which, however, are only noticeable upon closer inspection of the work. The text described a total of 93 illustration plates, although only 90 were printed. A plate is missing for Number XXXIX: "Montserrat Pine", for Number XLII: "Black Pine", and for Number XLVI: "Stiped Sugar-Loaf Pine." There is a note about this in the copy preserved in Vienna. Brookshaw originally wanted to prepare these three illustrations as well. But when he later decided on fewer pineapple varieties the enumeration for the other plates had already been set in print. Three other little caption plates are glued over and the number of another has been corrected. Finally, the descriptions of some varieties were printed in the wrong place. But the illustration numbers, which head each description, still allow proper assignment of the prints.

in London. Es wurden Kupferplatten mit unterschiedlicher Größe verwendet: Die Abmessungen der 13 kleineren Platten sind circa 410 x 310 mm, die der überwiegend größeren Platten circa 450 x 350 mm oder größer. Die jeweils bearbeitete Bildfläche stimmt bei allen Kupferplatten aber annähernd überein. Diesen Ausgleich erzielten die Stecher, indem sie die kleinen Kupferplatten vollständig bis zum Plattenrand bearbeiteten, hingegen bei den größeren Kupferplatten einen breiteren Randstreifen unbearbeitet ließen. Für die Anfertigung einer Druckplatte wurden zunächst nach Brookshaws Bildvorlage die Umrisse des Bildmotivs auf eine zurechtgeschnittene blanke Kupferplatte gezeichnet. Danach bedeckte man die Kupferplatte mit einer dünnen, säurefesten Firnisschicht an jenen Stellen, die erst später oder gar nicht bearbeitet wurden. Bei den Bildtafeln, die einen dunklen Hintergrund aufweisen, wurde die Aquatinta verwendet. Dieses Ätzverfahren benutzten die Stecher ebenso für die Gestaltung der Früchte, Blätter, Blüten, Stengel und Zweigausschnitte.

Für den Hintergrund wurden sehr winzige Staubkörner so auf der Kupferplatte fixiert, dass im anschließenden längeren bzw. mehrmaligen Säurebad die größeren Zwischenräume der frei gebliebenen Metallfläche tief geätzt werden konnten. All die winzigen Vertiefungen im Metall konnten soviel Druckfarbe aufnehmen, dass der Bildhintergrund letztendlich auf dem Papier als tiefer und satter Ton wirken kann. Hingegen wurden zum Beispiel für die zu gestaltenden Früchte oft Staubkörner unterschiedlicher Größe verschieden dicht auf die Kupferplatte gestreut und unterschiedlich tief geätzt, um die jeweilige Oberflächenstruktur der Früchte möglichst charakteristisch wiederzugeben. Auf diese Weise wurde auch die dreidimensionale Wirkung der abgebildeten Früchte erzielt. Um jedoch die scheinbare Echtheit vor allem der Früchte noch zu steigern, wendete Brookshaw mit seinen Mitarbeitern die Punktiermanier an. Gezielt konnten sie mit den spitzen oder abgeflachteren Nadeln des Rouletts die Kupferplatte bearbeiten. Nur unter der Lupe sind gleichmäßig aneinander gereihte Punkte oder auch kurze Stiche deutlich zu erkennen. Schließlich konnten die Stecher mit dem Grabstichel in der Technik des Kupferstichs einzelne schmale Grate aus dem Metall schneiden. Nach dem Drucken dienten diese Linien zur Betonung der Blattadern und der Konturen sowie als Schraffuren für die Schattierungen und Schattenwürfe. Das oftmals am unteren Rand mit einer Zierleiste umrandete Inschriftentäfelchen entstand ebenfalls in dieser Drucktechnik. Bei den Bildtafeln mit Ananasfrüchten, Weintrauben und Melonen ist der Verweis auf Brookshaws Tätigkeit auf dem unteren, nicht bearbeiteten Randbereich der Kupferplatte, zwischen Aquatinta und Plattenrand, angegeben. Da in diesen Fällen jeweils nur eine Frucht pro Tafel abgebildet ist, bot es sich an, den jeweiligen Sortennamen einzugravieren.

War die Übertragung eines Bildmotivs auf eine Kupferplatte beendet, so wurden die restliche Deckschicht entfernt und ein einfarbiger Probedruck durchgeführt. Anhand dieses so genannten Probeabzugs konnte Brookshaw die Qualität der bisher erreichten Arbeit und die Wirkung der Abbildung überprüfen. Durch diesen erstmalig auf die Kupferplatte ausgeübten starken Druck wurde auch der bearbeiteten Bildoberfläche ihre absolute Schärfe genommen. Danach bereitete man die Kupferplatte und das Papier mit dem Wasserzeichen J. WHATMAN für den ersten Druck vor. Die Druckfarben wurden mit Leinöl und Firnis zu einer zähen Konsistenz vermischt, denn sie sollten auf dem Papier nicht leicht zu verwischen sein. Mit Hilfe von Tampons oder mit Mull umwickelten Fingerspitzen wurden maximal drei Druckfarben jeweils gezielt auf vorher festgelegte Partien des Bildmotivs aufgetragen. Danach wischte der Drucker die Oberfläche der Kupferplatte sauber aus, so dass nur noch die Vertiefungen der Platte mit Farbe satt gefüllt waren. Der für Hintergrund und Inschrift gewählte Braunton wurde oftmals auch für die

que le fond de l'image apparût finalement sur le papier dans des tons riches et nourris. En revanche, pour les fruits par exemple, on répartissait sur les surfaces concernées des grains de poudre de taille variable, avec une densité qui était calculé en fonction de la profondeur de morsure nécessaire pour rendre aussi fidèlement que possible la structure superficielle caractéristique de chaque fruit. C'est ainsi que s'obtenait aussi l'effet tridimensionnel des fruits illustrés. Mais pour renforcer encore le sentiment d'apparente réalité, Brookshaw et ses collaborateurs appliquèrent en outre la technique du pointillé. A l'aide des pointes aiguës ou aplaties de leur roulette, ils pouvaient graver les plaques avec une très grande précision. Il faut une loupe pour voir clairement qu'il s'agit en fait d'une succession de points ou de traits. Pour finir, les graveurs découpaient dans le métal de fines ébarbures à l'aide d'un ciselet, selon la technique de la gravure sur cuivre. Après l'impression, les lignes ainsi tracées servaient à souligner les veines des feuilles et les contours, et à former les hachures pour les dégradés et les zones d'ombre. Le petit écriteau entouré d'une bordure décorative qui figure souvent en bas des planches était également réalisé dans cette technique. Sur les planches d'ananas, de raisins et de melons, la mention du rôle de Brookshaw est fréquemment indiquée dans la marge inférieure de la plaque de cuivre, entre l'aquatinte et le bord de plaque.

En effet, étant donnée la taille du fruit, il n'était possible d'en représenter qu'un spécimen par plaque, de sorte qu'il y avait assez de place pour graver le nom de la variété représentée. Une fois que le motif avait été transféré à la plaque, le reste de la couche de recouvrement était éliminé et une épreuve couleur imprimée. Celle-ci permettait à Brookshaw de vérifier la qualité du travail accompli et l'effet obtenu. Emoussés par la forte pression exercée sur la plaque lors de cette première épreuve, les traits perdaient un peu de leur netteté. Puis on préparait la plaque de cuivre et le papier en leur imprimant le filigrane J. WHATMAN. Les couleurs d'impression étaient mélangées à de l'huile de lin et à du vernis jusqu'à obtention d'une consistance épaisse pour qu'elles ne puissent pas s'effacer facilement sur le papier. Trois couleurs au plus étaient ensuite appliquées avec une grande précision sur les parties préalablement définies du motif, à l'aide de tampons, ou de la pointe des doigts, enveloppés de mousseline. Puis le graveur essuyait soigneusement la surface de la plaque, de sorte que seuls les creux étaient encore saturés de couleur.

Le ton brun choisi pour le fond était souvent repris pour les fruits, les fleurs, les tiges et parfois même les feuilles, lorsque celles-ci n'étaient pas imprimées en vert. Pour les fruits d'un rouge brillant, on n'employait pas du rouge mais un brun rouille. Comment était-ce possible ? La quantité de couleur introduite dans les minuscules sillons gravés dans la plaque variait avec leur profondeur et leur espacement, de sorte que la quantité de couleur déposée sur le papier et les tons qui en résultaient produisaient toutes sortes de nuances, dès le dépôt de la première couleur. Ensuite des coloristes, souvent d'ailleurs des femmes, appliquaient soigneusement différentes couleurs d'aquarelle au pinceau. Certaines étaient mélangées à du blanc couvrant. Une fois de plus, peu de couleurs étaient nécessaires à ce stade. Car une seule couleur d'aquarelle donnait toute une palette de nuances selon l'intensité de la couleur qui était mêlée à la couche d'impression. Ainsi la technique qui consiste à utiliser peu de couleurs d'impression et relativement peu de teintes d'aquarelle est un système extrêmement étudié permettant d'obtenir ces tons brillants, lumineux et flamboyants qui ravissent le lecteur.

Ce processus de réalisation de la *Pomona Britannica* a certainement exigé de la part de Brookshaw une concentration, une efficacité et un pouvoir de coordination considérables pour qu'il puisse mener à bien les multiples tâches nécessaires sur un temps aussi long. Quelques

6

A Fruit Piece – Still Life of Fruits and Flowers, 1781
Richard Earlom, colour mezzotint and etching after a painting by Jan van Huysum

Earlom's (1742/43–1822) brilliant graphic reproductions of Huysum's (1682–1749) still lifes, revealing both artistic and technical skill, were very popular during the 18th century. His fellow Englishmen particularly admired such meticulous depictions of fruits and flowers, aesthetically arranged as an ensemble.

A Fruit Piece – Stillleben mit Früchten und Blumen, 1781
Richard Earlom, Farbschabkunst und Radierung, nach einem Gemälde von Jan van Huysum

Earloms (1742/43–1822) künstlerisch-technisch brillante Reproduktionsgraphiken nach Huysums (1682–1749) Stillleben waren im 18. Jahrhundert sehr beliebt. Gern verweilten vor allem seine englischen Zeitgenossen vor solch akribisch dargestellten Früchten und Blumen, die zu einem ästhetischen Ensemble zusammengeführt sind.

A Fruit Piece – Nature morte avec fruits et fleurs, 1781
Gravure couleur à la manière noire et à l'eau-forte, de Richard Earlom, d'après un tableau de Jan van Huysum (1682–1749)

Les brillantes gravures de reproduction d'Earlom (1742/43–1822), qui excellaient à la fois sur les plans artistique et technique, avaient beaucoup d'amateurs au XVIIIᵉ siècle. Les contemporains, surtout en Angleterre, contemplaient avec plaisir ces représentations minutieuses de fruits et de fleurs, réunis en des compositions harmonieuses.

The large amount of work involved in each printing and the progressive wear on the copper plates permitted only a limited number of high-quality prints. That also explains the high purchase price, even for that time: in 1812 a complete copy, weighing about 13 kg, cost 59 pounds and 18 shillings. The number of impressions of the *Pomona Britannica* is not recorded. Besides complete copies, ones delivered in 30 separate installments were also available. The separate issues in particular tempted art dealers to remove illustrations for individual sale at a profit; such splendid separate sheets are being offered today more than ever before in the art market. Besides the complete copy presented here from the state collection of rare books and copperplate engravings in Greiz, only a few other complete editions have survived. They form a part of the following collections and libraries: the Staatsbibliothek zu Berlin – Preussischer Kulturbesitz in Berlin; the National Library in London; the New York Public Library; the Oak Spring Garden Library in Upperville, Virginia; the Library of Congress in Washington; and the Österreichische Nationalbibliothek in Vienna.

While it may well be tempting to take a look at one of these copies during a future visit to one of these cities, the exquisite originals suffer with each use, however careful, in a relentless process of deterioration. For this reason also the present reprint by TASCHEN is important: for the first time, almost two centuries after the appearance of the *Pomona Britannica* in London, all the illustrations are being made available to the general public in high-quality prints. Anyone who is not yet a lover of fruits has the best chance of becoming one now and of sharing with Brookshaw the fascination that "those blossoms which expanded in clusters with so much beauty – like harbingers proclaiming the return of spring – (should) now, by inscrutable changes, decorate (… the) table with the most delightful repasts" (ill. 6).

7

Pomona Britannica, Plate | Tafel | Planche XL
Black Jamaica Pine

The development of illustrated pomological works – feasts for the eye

The spectrum of plants depicted in botanical works since the end of the 17th century had grown enormously compared with those found in herbals of the 16th and 17th centuries. Herbs of mainly medicinal significance were now accompanied by pharmaceutically useless plants, wild plants and cultivated varieties. Fruits, too, were presented with greater care. The woodcut was increasingly abandoned as a means of reproducing plant illustrations and eventually the copperplate engraving replaced it completely. The growing number of research expeditions since the end of the 17th century, on which numerous plant varieties were discovered, led to increased knowledge of the subject. Newly established or developed botanical gardens provided another copious source of plant material. Finally, naturalists and gardeners were joined by contemporaries primarily of more privileged backgrounds, who devoted their leisure time to growing fruits and cultivating new varieties. One precursor of the science of botany, which was only established a century later, was Joseph Pitton de Tournefourt (1656–1708), a member of the Académie des Sciences in Paris and professor at the Jardin du Roi, the royal gardens in the French capital. His 1694 publication, *Eléments de botanique* – appearing from 1700 in Latin translation under the title *Institutiones rei herbariae* – already contains precise depictions of different varieties of fruits along with separate details.

In the first quarter of the 18th century, the preoccupation with cultivating and classifying fruits began to become more pronounced. One of the many works worth mentioning from England is the *Gardeners Dictionary* (1731) by Philip Miller (1691–1771). He was a respected naturalist and gardener at the Physic Garden in Chelsea, whose acclaimed horticultural reference reached its eighth edition in 1768, with trans-

Früchte, Blüten, Stengel und manchmal sogar für die Blätter genutzt, falls letztere nicht in Grün gedruckt werden sollten. Für sehr rot leuchtende Früchte wurde nicht etwa Rot, sondern Rostbraun verwendet. Wie war das möglich? Je nach Tiefe der geätzten winzigen Partien und deren Abstand zueinander wurde unterschiedlich viel Druckfarbe aufgenommen, womit auch die aufs Papier abgegebene Farbmenge und dementsprechend der Farbton verschieden ausfallen konnten. Daraus resultierte, dass selbst bei einer einzigen Druckfarbe sich nuancierte Farbtöne auf dem Papier ergaben. Anschließend trugen die Koloristen, bei denen es sich oftmals um Frauen handelte, sorgfältig mit dem Pinsel verschiedene Wasserfarben auf. Teilweise wurden die Wasserfarben mit Deckweiß ausgemischt. Auch bei diesem Arbeitsschritt waren relativ wenige Farben erforderlich, denn eine Wasserfarbe ergab in Verbindung mit einer Druckfarbe je nach deren Intensität unterschiedliche Farbtöne. Diese Farbpalette konnte erweitert werden durch die jeweilige Wasserfarbenintensität, die durch das Mischungsverhältnis von Wasser und Farbpartikeln bestimmt wurde. Fazit: Das Drucken mit wenigen Farben und das Kolorieren mit relativ wenigen Wasserfarben ist ein äußerst ausgetüfteltes System, durch das letztendlich jene schimmernden, leuchtenden und glühend-feurigen Farbtöne erzielt werden, die den Betrachter entzücken.

Mit Sicherheit erforderte der Entstehungsprozess der *Pomona Britannica* gerade von Brookshaw Enormes an Konzentration, Leistungsfähigkeit und Koordinationsvermögen, damit er die vielfältigen Arbeiten über die längere Zeit zum gelungenen Abschluss bringen konnte. Während dieser Periode traten kleinere Pannen und Versehen auf, die jedoch nur bei genauer Betrachtung des Werkes auffallen. Im Text werden insgesamt 93 Bildtafeln beschrieben, von denen jedoch nur 90 gedruckt sind. Es fehlen die Tafeln zu Nummer XXXIX: „Montserrat Pine", Nummer XLII: „Black Pine" und Nummer XLVI: „Stiped Sugar-Loaf Pine". In dem in Wien aufbewahrten Druckexemplar befindet sich hierzu ein Verweis. Brookshaw wollte ursprünglich auch diese drei Abbildungen anfertigen. Als er sich später jedoch für die kleinere Anzahl der Ananassorten entschieden hatte, war die Nummerierung für die anderen Tafeln bereits per Druck festgelegt. Auch sind drei Inschriftentäfelchen überklebt und bei einem weiteren ist die Nummer korrigiert. Schließlich sind einige Beschreibungen der Sorten an falscher Stelle gedruckt. Sie können aber durch die darüber stehende Abbildungsnummer den entsprechenden Drucken zugeordnet werden.

Die für jeden erneuten Druck aufzuwendende hohe Arbeit und die dabei stets fortschreitende Abnutzung der Kupferplatten ließ nur eine begrenzte Anzahl von hervorragenden Drucken zu. Aus diesem Grund erklärt sich auch der für damalige Verhältnisse hohe Kaufpreis: Im Jahre 1812 kostete ein vollständiges, circa 13 kg schweres Exemplar 59 britische Pfund und 18 Shilling. In welcher Auflage die *Pomona Britannica* gedruckt wurde, ist nicht belegt. Neben dem vollständigen Exemplar wurden auch 30 Teillieferungen angeboten. Gerade bei den Teillieferungen schreckten Kunsthändler nicht davor zurück, Abbildungen zu entnehmen, um sie einzeln Gewinn bringend zu verkaufen. Heute mehr denn je werden die prachtvollen Einzelblätter auf dem Kunstmarkt angeboten und neben dem hier vorgestellten Exemplar aus der Staatlichen Bücher- und Kupferstichsammlung in Greiz sind nur noch wenige vollständige Exemplare in Sammlungen und Bibliotheken erhalten, unter anderem in: Berlin, Staatsbibliothek zu Berlin – Preußischer Kulturbesitz; London, National Library; New York, New York Public Library; Upperville Virginia, Oak Spring Garden Library; Washington, Library of Congress und Wien, Österreichische Nationalbibliothek.

Nun mag es sehr verlockend sein, sich beim nächsten Aufenthalt in einer dieser Städte ein Druckexemplar im Original anzusehen. Doch mit

petites pannes et erreurs, qui n'apparaissent pas à première vue, se sont cependant produites pendant cette période de travail. Le texte décrit au total 93 planches alors que seules 90 sont imprimées ; il manque les planches numéro XXXIX « Montserrat Pine, numéro XLII « Black Pine » et numéro XLVI « Stiped Sugar-Loaf Pine ». Dans l'exemplaire imprimé conservé à Vienne, une indication est donnée à ce sujet. Brookshaw avait eu tout d'abord l'intention de réaliser ces trois planches. Mais quand il décida finalement de les supprimer, la numérotation des autres planches avait déjà été gravée sur les plaques d'impression. Trois écriteaux sont recouverts et dans un autre, un numéro a été corrigé. Enfin quelques descriptions de variétés sont imprimées au mauvais endroit, mais il est facile de trouver les planches correspondantes grâce à leur numéro.

Etant donné le travail colossal nécessité par chaque impression et l'usure progressive des plaques de cuivre, il n'a été possible d'imprimer qu'un nombre limité d'ouvrages de très grande qualité. C'est ce qui explique le prix très élevé pour l'époque : en 1812, un exemplaire complet, d'environ 13 kg, coûtait 59 livres anglaises et 18 shillings. Nous ne connaissons pas le tirage de la *Pomona Britannica*. Il y eut aussi 30 exemplaires partiels, dont les marchands d'art n'hésitaient pas à détacher des illustrations pour les vendre séparément avec profit. Aujourd'hui, ces feuilles exceptionnelles sont plus que jamais proposées sur le marché de l'art, de sorte que les exemplaires complets sont rares. Outre le présent ouvrage, qui provient de la Collection nationale de livres et de gravures de Greiz, on peut notamment citer ceux de Berlin, Nationalbibliothek-Preussischer Kulturbesitz ; de Londres, National Library ; de New York, New York Public Library ; d'Upperville Virginia, Oak Spring Garden Library ; de Washington, Library of Congress et de Vienne, Bibliothèque nationale d'Autriche.

Il peut être très tentant d'aller consulter l'un de ces ouvrages lors d'un prochain séjour dans une de ces villes. Mais chaque nouvelle consultation, aussi attentionnée soit-elle, détériore un peu plus l'état de ces merveilleux originaux. C'est l'une des raisons qui rendent la réimpression de ce livre par les éditions TASCHEN aussi précieuse : près de deux siècles après la parution de la *Pomona Britannica* à Londres, toutes les illustrations de l'œuvre originale seront pour la première fois mises à disposition du grand public avec une qualité d'impression excellente. Ceux qui ne sont pas encore des amateurs de fruits ont toutes les chances de le devenir et pourront partager la fascination de Brookshaw, qui s'extasiait devant : « (…) ces fleurs, signes avant-coureurs de la venue du printemps. Elles se déploient en grappes avec tant de beauté (…) [et] décorent maintenant, à la suite d'une mystérieuse métamorphose, (… la) table des mets les plus délicieux » (ill. 6).

La création d'ouvrages pomologiques illustrés – un plaisir esthétique

Depuis la fin du XVIIe siècle, le nombre de plantes représentées dans les manuels de botanique s'était considérablement accru par rapport à celui des livres d'herboristerie des XVIe et XVIIe siècles. A côté des essences médicinales, on y trouvait désormais des plantes sauvages ou cultivées, sans intérêt pharmaceutique particulier. De même, les espèces de fruits et leurs nombreuses variétés y étaient beaucoup plus représentées. L'usage de la gravure sur bois déclina peu à peu, pour finalement céder entièrement le pas à la gravure sur cuivre. Cet élargissement des connaissances était dû d'une part au nombre croissant de voyages entrepris depuis la fin du XVIIe siècle pour découvrir et explorer de nombreuses plantes. D'autre part, avec l'extension et la multiplication des jardins botaniques, les chercheurs disposaient d'un important matériel végétal. Enfin, l'époque comptait aussi, outre les naturalistes et les

lations into French, Dutch and German. At that time the Dutch horticulturist and mathematician Johann Herrmann Knoop (1700–1769) published a number of treatises specifically on varieties of fruits. His two-part *Pomologia* also appeared in an expanded German edition (1760–1766). The author's purpose was to describe and depict the best varieties of apples, pears, cherries and plums grown at that time mainly in Holland, Germany, France and England. Each of the 44 handcoloured copperplate engravings illustrates and names at least eight varieties of a species of fruit (ill. 9).

In 1768 a Frenchman of many interests, Henri Louis Duhamel du Monceau (1700–1782), published his *Traité des arbres fruitiers*. This botanist and naval engineer provided the first comprehensive descriptions of specific fruit characteristics in this outstanding work and included accurate depictions of them in 180 copperplate engravings. Duhamel du Monceau's efforts transformed fruit growing and cultivation into a recognized scientific subdiscipline of applied botany. The French Revolution put a temporary stop to such research, but detailed inventories of fruits cultivated in France, Holland, Austria, Switzerland and Germany were still published before 1800.

Horticultural and pomological works proposing to introduce every type of fruit along with their varieties were supplemented by specific studies on individual species. *Ananas. A treatise on the Pineapple* from 1767, was one written by the English horticulturist John Giles (c. 1726–1797). Johann Simon Kerner (1755–1830), a German naturalist, teacher of botany, and supervisor of the botanical gardens in Stuttgart, published a rare and magnificent work about grapes that appeared in 12 installments from 1803 to 1815, containing 144 watercolour paintings of as many grape varieties from the whole world (ill. 8). Pomological inquiries were not limited to France, England and Holland. In Austria the first part of the *Abhandlung von den Obstbäumen* in ten issues appeared between 1787 and 1792 by the nurseryman Johann Kraft (d. 1797). This now rare work presents varieties of fruits cultivated in his "imperially privileged" tree nursery in Weinhaus, just outside Vienna. A brief description of the varieties, their raising and tending, is illuminated by 100 carefully handcoloured copperplate engravings recording simply but accurately the specific characteristics of the fruits, blossoms and leaves.

In Germany the pastor and pomologist Johann Volkmar Sickler (1742–1820) from Thuringia was one of the leading specialists on fruits. Having edited the journal *Der teutsche Obstgärtner* (1794–1804) in Weimar (ill. 10), he was instrumental in establishing the successor periodical *Allgemeines Teutsches Garten-Magazin* (1804–1817). There, too, detailed descriptions of new and productive native and foreign fruit varieties were provided with simple depictions, often accurately painted copperplate engravings: an example illustrates the then popular gooseberry varieties from England (ill. 11). His interesting publications and many successes in his nursery earned Sickler membership in the Horticultural Society of London and the Academy of Sciences in Erfurt. From the late 18th century onward, model fruits of wax, plaster or similar materials were made as an additional pomological resource in many European countries. Under Sickler's direction the *Pomologische Kabinett* was established in collaboration with Friedrich Justin Bertuch (1747–1822), publisher of the Landes-Industrie-Comptoir in Weimar. This collection of about 300 naturalistic wax models of fruits included 104 varieties each of apples and pears, 38 of cherries, 35 of plums and damsons and 15 varieties of peaches. A considerable number of these wax fruits, which are certainly worth a visit, are now to be found among the possessions of the Kulturstiftung Wörlitz-Dessau and the holdings of the Naturkunde Museum in Bamberg.

jeder erneuten, noch so vorsichtigen Einsicht wird der Zustand dieser exquisiten Originale in einem schleichenden Prozess negativ beeinträchtigt. Auch deshalb ist dieser Reprint des TASCHEN-Verlags bedeutsam: Beinahe zwei Jahrhunderte nach dem Erscheinen der *Pomona Britannica* in London werden erstmals alle darin enthaltenen Abbildungen in hervorragender Druckqualität einem großen Publikum zur Verfügung gestellt. Wer bis jetzt noch kein Liebhaber von Früchten ist, hat die besten Chancen, einer zu werden und kann mit Brookshaw die Faszination teilen, dass „(…) jene Blüten, die sich mit so viel Schönheit in Gruppen entfalten – wie Vorboten die Rückkehr des Frühlings ankündigen – nun durch unergründliche Wandlungen (… den) Tisch mit den herrlichsten Mahlzeiten dekorieren." (Abb. 6)

Die Entwicklung pomologischer Abbildungswerke – ein ästhetischer Genuss

Seit dem Ende des 17. Jahrhunderts hatte sich das Spektrum der dargestellten Pflanzen in botanischen Abhandlungen gegenüber jenem in den Kräuterbüchern des 16. und 17. Jahrhunderts enorm erweitert. Neben den ehemals hauptsächlich arzneilich nutzbaren Pflanzen waren nun auch pharmazeutisch belanglose, wild wachsende wie auch kultivierte Pflanzen präsent. Entsprechend intensiver wurden auch Obstarten mit ihren Sorten vorgestellt. Zur Vervielfältigung von Pflanzenabbildungen wurde der Holzschnitt immer seltener verwendet und schließlich vom Kupferstich gänzlich abgelöst. Die Wissenserweiterung resultierte einerseits aus den zunehmenden Forschungsreisen seit dem Ende des 17. Jahrhunderts, auf denen zahlreiche Pflanzen entdeckt wurden. Andererseits stand durch die Neugründungen und den Ausbau botanischer Gärten umfangreiches Pflanzenmaterial zur Verfügung. Schließlich gab es neben den Naturforschern und Gärtnern auch jene, vor allem gut betuchten Zeitgenossen, die sich in ihrer Freizeit mit dem Obstbau und den Obstsorten beschäftigten. Ein früher Vorläufer der sich um 1800 als Wissenschaft etablierenden Botanik war Joseph Pitton de Tournefourt (1656–1708), Mitglied der Académie des Sciences zu Paris und Professor am Jardin du Roi, dem Garten der Könige von Frankreich in Paris. Sein 1694 veröffentlichtes Werk *Eléments de botanique* – unter dem Titel *Institutiones rei herbariae* ab 1700 in lateinischer Übersetzung erschienen – enthält bereits exakte Abbildungen von verschiedenen Obstarten mit separaten Details.

Seit dem ersten Viertel des 18. Jahrhunderts ist eine intensivere Beschäftigung mit dem Obstbau und den Obstsorten zu verzeichnen. In England leistete unter anderem Philip Miller (1691–1771) in seinem *Gardeners dictionary* (1731) einen nennenswerten Beitrag. Als angesehener Naturforscher und Gärtner im Physic Garden in Chelsea konnte er sein gefeiertes Nachschlagewerk über den Gartenbau bis 1768 in acht Auflagen, auch in Französisch, Holländisch und Deutsch, herausgeben. Zu jener Zeit verfasste der holländische Gärtner und Mathematiker Johann Herrmann Knoop (1700–1769) mehrere Abhandlungen speziell über Obstsorten. In seiner zweiteiligen, auch als erweiterte deutschsprachige Ausgabe erschienenen *Pomologia* (1760–1766) sind die besten Sorten der Äpfel, Birnen, Kirschen und Pflaumen beschrieben und abgebildet, die damals vor allem in Holland, Deutschland, Frankreich und England wuchsen. Auf jedem der 44 kolorierten Kupferstiche sind mindestens acht Sorten einer Obstart mit Angabe ihrer Namen dargestellt (Abb. 9).

Im Jahre 1768 gab der vielseitig interessierte, als Botaniker und Marinetechniker tätige Franzose Henri Louis Duhamel du Monceau (1700–1782) seinen *Traité des arbres fruitiers* heraus. In diesem hervorragenden Obstwerk sind die spezifischen Kennzeichen der Früchte erstmals umfassend definiert und auf 180 präzisen Kupferstichen abgebildet. Durch Duhamel du Monceaus Schaffen wurde die Beschäftigung mit

jardiniers, des personnes fortunées qui s'adonnaient, dans leurs loisirs, à la culture des fruits et au développement des variétés. La botanique, qui devint une discipline scientifique vers 1800, eut un précurseur en la personne de Joseph Pitton de Tournefort (1656–1708), membre de l'Académie des sciences de Paris et professeur au Jardin du Roi. Son ouvrage, *Eléments de botanique* – publié en 1694 et paru en latin à partir de 1700 sous le titre *Institutiones rei herbariae* – contient déjà des reproductions exactes de différentes sortes de fruits avec leurs détails distinctifs.

Depuis le premier quart du XVIIIe siècle, on note un travail intensif sur la culture des fruits et la découverte des variétés. En Angleterre, Philip Miller (1691–1771), entre autres, apporta une contribution remarquable avec son *Gardeners Dictionary* (1731). Ses travaux au Physic Garden de Chelsea ont permis à ce naturaliste et jardinier estimé de publier un ouvrage de référence sur l'horticulture très bien accueilli, qui connut huit éditions, dont celles en français, en hollandais et en allemand. A la même époque, le jardinier et mathématicien hollandais, Johann Herrmann Knoop (1700–1769), écrivit plusieurs manuels consacrés exclusivement aux variétés de fruits. Dans sa *Pomologia* (1760–1766) en deux parties, dont il existe une version augmentée en langue allemande, l'auteur décrit et illustre ce qu'il considère comme étant les meilleures variétés de pommes, poires, cerises et prunes qui poussaient à l'époque en Hollande, en Allemagne, en France et en Angleterre. Chacune des 44 gravures sur cuivre coloriées regroupe au moins huit sortes d'une même espèce de fruit, avec indication de leur nom (ill. 9).

En 1768, Henri Louis Duhamel du Monceau (1700–1782), un Français aux multiples centres d'intérêt, qui exerçait entre autres les métiers de botaniste et de technicien de la marine, publia un *Traité des arbres fruitiers*. Cet excellent ouvrage consacré aux fruits décrit pour la première fois de manière exhaustive les caractéristiques spécifiques de chaque variété et les reproduit avec précision en 180 gravures sur cuivre. L'activité de Duhamel du Monceau conféra aux travaux sur la culture des fruits et sur les différentes variétés une reconnaissance scientifique, de sorte que ce domaine devint une sous-discipline de la botanique appliquée. Les recherches françaises sur les fruits furent interrompues pendant la Révolution, mais encore avant le tournant du XIXe siècle, des listes détaillées sur les fruits cultivés en France, en Hollande, en Autriche, en Suisse et en Allemagne furent de nouveau publiées.

Outre ces ouvrages sur l'horticulture et les fruits, qui s'évertuaient à présenter le plus grand nombre possible d'espèces de fruits et de variétés, des monographies consacrées à une seule espèce parurent également. Le jardinier anglais John Giles (vers 1726–1797) avait par exemple publié en 1767 une étude sur l'ananas: *Ananas. A treatise on the Pineapple*.

Johann Simon Kerner (1755–1830), un naturaliste allemand, professeur de botanique et superviseur du jardin botanique de Stuttgart, publia en 12 parties, entre 1803 et 1815, un superbe ouvrage sur le raisin, qui contenait 144 aquarelles correspondant au même nombre de variétés de raisin découvertes dans le monde entier (ill. 8).

Des études pomologiques furent menées non seulement en France, en Angleterre, en Hollande mais aussi en Autriche. De 1787 à 1792 parut en 10 cahiers la première partie d'un traité sur les arbres fruitiers, *Abhandlung von den Obstbäumen*, du pépiniériste autrichien Johann Kraft (mort en 1797). Dans cet ouvrage, aujourd'hui très rare, Kraft présentait des variétés de fruits qu'il cultivait dans sa pépinière de Weinhaus, aux portes de Vienne, et pour laquelle il avait les faveurs de l'empereur. A côté de courtes descriptions, variété par variété, de leur

Bacchus presenting Grapes to Pomona, 1803
Unknown artist, watercolour with opaque white from J.S. Kerner's *Le Raisin*

This frontispiece of the first edition is a homage to the viticulture of antiquity: descending on a cloud, Bacchus, the god of wine and ecstasy, is giving Pomona, the goddess of fruits and gardening, a plump bunch of grapes for her cornucopia of fruits.

Bacchus schenkt Pomona eine Weinrebe, 1803
Unkannter Künstler. Wasserfarben und Deckweiß, aus J.S. Kerners *Le Raisin*

Das Titelbild der ersten Ausgabe ist eine Hommage an die antike Weinkultur: Der auf einer Wolke herabschwebende Bacchus, Gott des Weines und der Ekstase, schenkt Pomona, Göttin der Früchte und des Obstbaus, eine saftige Weinrebe für ihr Früchte-Füllhorn.

Bacchus offrant une grappe de raisins à Pomona, 1803
Artiste inconnu, aquarelle et gouache de *Le Raisin* de J.S. Kerner

Le frontispice de la 1re édition est un hommage à l'antique culture du vin: Bacchus, dieu du vin et de l'extase, descendant dans les airs sur un nuage, offre à Pomona, déesse des fruits et de la culture fruitière, une grappe juteuse pour sa corne d'abondance.

Eight apple varieties: Golden Double-Sweet, Hollow Sweet Gray, Winter Blossom Sweet, Golden Simple, Double-Gray Golden, Red Crown or Agate Apple, Kantjes Apple, Sweet Crown Apple, 1760
Unknown artist, copperplate engraving, subsequently coloured, from J.H. Knoop's *Pomologia*

This loose array of apples does not render the specific surface structures and colours of the peels as precisely or with such aesthetic appeal as in pomological illustrations of succeeding decades.

Acht Apfelsorten: Golden Double-Sweet, Hollow Sweet Gray, Winter Blossom Sweet, Golden Simple, Double-Gray Golden, Red Crown or Agate Apple, Kantjes Apple, Sweet Crown Apple, 1760
Unbekannter Künstler, Kupferstich, nachträglich koloriert, aus J.H. Knoops *Pomologia*

Bei den locker arrangierten Apfelsorten sind die spezifischen Oberflächenstrukturen und Farben der Fruchtschalen noch nicht so präzise und ästhetisch ansprechend wiedergegeben wie in den pomologischen Abbildungen der folgenden Jahrzehnte.

Huit sortes de fruits: Golden Double-Sweet, Hollow Sweet Gray, Winter Blossom Sweet, Golden Simple, Double-Gray Golden, Red Crown or Agate Apple, Kantjes Apple, Sweet Crown Apple, 1760
Artiste inconnu, gravure sur cuivre, coloriée ultérieurement, de la *Pomologia* de J.H. Knoop

Sur ces variétés de pommes librement disposées, les structures de surface spécifiques et la couleur des peaux ne sont pas encore rendues avec autant de précision et de charme esthétique que dans les reproductions pomologiques des décennies suivantes.

Double Portrait of Ferdinand von Könitz and Baron Christian von Truchsess, 1800
C. Westermayr, aquatint and copperplate engraving

This double portrait of the Franconian pomologists was appropriately adorned with two fruit-laden branches: Könitz (1756–1832, front left) was mainly a breeder of pears and his friend Truchsess was known as an avid cultivator of cherries. It was Könitz, incidentally, who suggested to Sickler that the periodical *Der teutsche Obstgärtner* arrange to have model fruits made of wax.

10

Doppelporträt Ferdinand von Könitz und Christian Freiherr von Truchsess, 1800. C. Westermayr, Aquatinta und Kupferstich
Das Doppelporträt der fränkischen Pomologen wurde mit zwei Fruchtzweigen trefflich verziert: Könitz (1756–1832, links vorn) war vor allem Birnenzüchter und sein Freund Truchsess galt als eifriger Kirschenzüchter. Übrigens war es Könitz, der Sickler die Anfertigung von Wachsfrüchten für die Zeitschrift *Der teutsche Obstgärtner* vorschlug.

Double portrait de Ferdinand von Könitz et Christian baron de Truchsess, 1800. Aquatinte et gravure sur cuivre de C. Westermayr
Ce double portrait de deux pomologues franconiens a été admirablement décoré à l'aide de deux branches de fruits : Könitz (1756–1832, devant, à gauche) cultivait surtout des poires et son ami Truchsess pratiquait activement la culture de cerises. Ce fut Könitz qui proposa à Sickler de réaliser des fruits en cire pour sa revue *Der teutsche Obstgärtner*.

Two English gooseberry varieties – Joyes Large White Gooseberries. Smith's Yellow Sporkels, 1804
Unknown aritist, copper engraving, stippled, painted in watercolour with opaque white, highlighting using natural resin

"In England gooseberries are now a kind of fad fruit" Sickler informed the readers of the *Allgemeines Teutsches Garten-Magazin*, and presented the best varieties in the pre-photographic era as softly painted copperplate engravings – a delight for pomologists and art-lovers alike.

11

Zwei englische Stachelbeersorten: Joyes weisse grosse Stachelbeere, Smith's gelbe Sporkels, 1804
Künstler unbekannt, Kupferstich, Punktiermanier, koloriert mit Wasserfarben und Deckweiß, Glanzlichter durch pflanzliches Harz

„In England ist jetzt die Stachelbeere eine Art von Modefrucht", teilte Sickler den Lesern des *Allgemeinen Teutschen Garten-Magazins* mit und präsentierte die besten Sorten im vorfotografischen Zeitalter als zart kolorierte Kupferstiche – ein Genuss für Pomologen wie Kunstliebhaber.

Grande groseille à maquereau blanche de Joye. Sporkels jaunes de Smith – Deux espèces anglaises de groseilles à maquereau, 1804
Artiste inconnu, gravure sur cuivre en pointillé. Coloriée à l'aquarelle et à la gouache blanche. Petits effets de lumière dus à la résine végétale

« En Angleterre, la groseille à maquereau est devenu une sorte de mode », confie Sickler à ses lecteurs du *Allgemeines Teutsches Garten-Magazin*, auxquels il présentait les meilleures variétés, dans ses gravures sur cuivre aux coloris délicats : à l'ère pré-photographique, un régal pour les pomologues et les amateurs d'art.

A remarkable rise in the number of periodicals about gardening and fruit growing went hand in hand with the establishment of many important horticultural clubs and associations from the beginning of the 19th century. The Horticultural Society founded in 1804 in London (since 1861 Royal Horticultural Society) played a major role in pomological science. One of its seven founding members was Sir Joseph Banks (1743–1819), a successful scientific consultant and honorary director of the Royal Botanic Gardens at Kew as well as president of that world-famous scientific association, the Royal Society of London. Fruit collections were planted in the gardens of the Horticultural Society in Chiswick with the goal of clarifying once and for all ambiguous classifications or identifications of the varieties. Old and new varieties originating from every region of the British Isles and Europe were studied. Members were encouraged to look for new varieties or to breed some themselves. In addition, they were invited to provide information and offer recommendations about individual fruit varieties and their cultivation, with the aim of improving the quality and assortment of fruits produced in Britain.

William Forsyth (1737–1804), royal gardener in Kensington and founding member of the Horticultural Society, published *A Treatise on the Culture and Management of Fruittrees*, which also appeared in a German edition (ills. 12 and 13). Live specimens were made available to society members and specialists abroad. Scions of robust apple varieties survived the long voyage to the American continent and, having arrived in Annapolis valley, became the original stock of the Nova Scotian and Canadian apple industries. The fruit expert Robert Thompson was able to identify more than 1200 apple varieties for the London Society's first *Catalogue of Fruits in the Garden of the Horticultural Society*, dating from 1826, although more than 400 varieties still lacked official nomenclature. Five years later, 1396 precisely named apple varieties were inventoried. Finally, Thompson co-published the accurately illustrated *Pomological Magazine* (1828–1830) with John Lindley (1799–1865), another member of the Horticultural Society and professor of botany at University College, London. This periodical provided thorough descriptions and evaluations of the commonest native and foreign apples, subdivided into eating and cooking varieties.

The emergence of luxurious pomonas at the beginning of the 19th century must be seen in connection with the boom in pomological studies. These generally very large books issued in small print-runs contain some of the most enchanting pictures of fruits ever made. Even though their relevance was primarily scientific, their aesthetic value must also be emphasized. More than mere illustrations, they were, indeed, works of art. The splendid depictions, which quite dominated their descriptive texts, were produced by the latest graphic techniques of stippling and aquatint. In France a completely revised edition of Duhamel du Monceau's *Traité des arbres fruitiers* (1768) appeared under the same title in separate installments between 1807 and 1835. This comprehensive work was compiled jointly by Pierre-Antoine Poiteau (1766–1854), botanist and director of the nursery at Versailles, and Pierre Jean François Turpin (1775–1840), botanist and plant physiologist. It was embellished with plates of exceptional artistic merit, including, for instance, depictions of 108 varieties of pears, 57 of apples, 49 of plums and 29 of cherries.

In 1811, one year before the appearance of the *Pomona Britannica* by George Brookshaw, the *Pomona Herefordiensis* was published. Its author, Thomas Andrew Knight (1759–1839), since 1810 president of the Horticultural Society, was able to engage a pomological illustrator of importance in England at the time for the 30 plates: William Hooker (1779–1832). The handcoloured aquatints depict primarily tried and

dem Obstbau und den Obstsorten als ein wissenschaftlicher Teilbereich der angewandten Botanik anerkannt. Die französischen Obst-Studien kamen zwar während der Französischen Revolution zum Erliegen, aber noch vor 1800 wurden wieder detaillierte Bestandslisten der in Frankreich, Holland, Österreich, Schweiz und Deutschland kultivierten Früchte publiziert.

Neben jenen Gartenbau- und Obstwerken, in denen möglichst viele Obstarten mit ihren jeweiligen Sorten vorgestellt wurden, erschienen auch spezielle Abhandlungen zu lediglich einer Art. Vom englischen Gärtner John Giles (um 1726–1797) lag zum Beispiel 1767 die Studie *Ananas. A treatise on the Pineapple* vor. Johann Simon Kerner (1755–1830), deutscher Naturwissenschaftler, Botaniklehrer und Aufseher des botanischen Gartens in Stuttgart, gab von 1803 bis 1815 in zwölf Lieferungen ein seltenes und prachtvolles Werk über Weintrauben heraus, dass 144 Wasserfarbenmalereien von ebenso vielen Traubensorten aus der ganzen Welt enthält (Abb. 8). Nicht nur in Frankreich, England und Holland, sondern auch in Österreich wurden pomologische Untersuchungen durchgeführt. Von 1787 bis 1792 erschien in zehn Heften der erste Teil der *Abhandlung von den Obstbäumen* vom Baumschulgärtner Johann Kraft (gest. 1797). In diesem heute sehr seltenen Werk werden Obstsorten vorgestellt, die Kraft in seiner kaiserlich privilegierten Baumschule in Weinhaus, vor den Stadttoren Wiens, kultivierte. Neben der kurzen Beschreibung der Sorten, ihrer Aufzucht und Pflege befinden sich 100 sorgfältig kolorierte Kupferstiche, auf denen in einer schlichten, aber sehr akkuraten Weise die spezifischen Merkmale der Früchte, Blüten und Blätter festgehalten sind.

In Deutschland war der Thüringer Pfarrer und Pomologe Johann Volkmar Sickler (1742–1820) einer der führenden Obstspezialisten. Nachdem er in Weimar bereits die Zeitschrift *Der teutsche Obstgärtner* (1794–1804) herausgegeben hatte (Abb. 10), war er maßgeblich an der Nachfolgezeitschrift *Allgemeines Teutsches Garten-Magazin* (1804–1817) beteiligt. Darin wurden auch neue und leistungsfähige, einheimische und ausländische Obstsorten ausführlich beschrieben und in schlicht gestochenen, oftmals präzise kolorierten Kupferstichen abgebildet, zum Beispiel die damals beliebten Stachelbeersorten aus England (Abb. 11). Sickler wurde für seine interessanten Publikationen und Erfolge in seiner Baumschule als Mitglied der Horticultural Society in London und der Akademie der Wissenschaften zu Erfurt ausgezeichnet. Um die Beschreibungen und Abbildungen von Fruchtsorten zu ergänzen, wurden seit dem späten 18. Jahrhundert in vielen Ländern Europas Modellfrüchte aus Wachs, Gips oder anderen Materialien hergestellt. Unter der Leitung von Sickler entstand in Zusammenarbeit mit Friedrich Justin Bertuch (1747–1822), Verleger des Landes-Industrie-Comptoir in Weimar, das *Pomologische Kabinett*. Diese Sammlung von circa 300 naturgetreuen Wachsmodellen von Früchten umfasste unter anderem je 104 Apfel- und Birnensorten, 38 Kirschsorten, 35 Pflaumen- und Zwetschgensorten sowie 15 Pfirsichsorten. Eine umfangreiche und sehenswerte Anzahl dieser Wachsfrüchte befindet sich heute im Eigentum der Kulturstiftung Wörlitz-Dessau sowie im Naturkunde-Museum in Bamberg.

Neben der seit Beginn des 19. Jahrhunderts zu verzeichnenden Zunahme von Zeitschriften zum Garten- und Obstbau wurden auch mehrere bedeutende Gartenbauvereine und Gartenbaugesellschaften gegründet. Einen wichtigen pomologischen Beitrag leistete die 1804 in London gegründete Horticultural Society (seit 1861 Royal Horticultural Society). Zu den sieben Gründungsmitgliedern zählte auch Sir Joseph Banks (1743–1819): erfolgreicher wissenschaftlicher Berater und inoffizieller Leiter des Royal Botanic Garden in Kew sowie Präsident der Royal Society in London, jener weltberühmten wissenschaftlichen Gesellschaft. In den Gärten der Horticultural Society in Chiswick wurden

culture et des soins à apporter, on trouve 100 gravures sur cuivre coloriées avec soin et montrant avec sobriété et précision les caractéristiques de chaque fruit, de ses fleurs et de ses feuilles.

En Allemagne, le curé de Thuringe, Johann Volkmar Sickler (1742–1820), était pomologue et l'un des plus grands spécialistes de fruits. Après avoir publié à Weimar la revue *Der teutsche Obstgärtner* (1794–1804) (ill. 10), il participa activement à la revue qui lui succéda, *Allgemeines Teutsches Garten-Magazin* (1804–1817). On y trouvait des descriptions détaillées de nouvelles sortes de fruits à bon rendement, cultivées dans le pays ou à l'étranger. Elles étaient reproduites sur des gravures sur cuivre sobres et souvent coloriées avec précision. Un exemple en sont les groseilles à maquereau d'Angleterre, très appréciées à l'époque (ill. 11). Membre de la Horticultural Society de Londres et de l'Académie des sciences d'Erfurt, Sickler reçut des distinctions pour ses publications intéressantes et ses succès de pépiniériste. Pour compléter toutes ces descriptions et illustrations, des modèles de fruits étaient réalisés en cire, en plâtre et en d'autres matériaux dans beaucoup de pays d'Europe à partir de la fin du XVIIIᵉ siècle. Sickler créa aussi, avec la collaboration de Friedrich Justin Bertuch (1747–1822), éditeur du Landes-Industrie-Comptoir à Weimar, un cabinet de pomologie, le *Pomologische Kabinett*. Cette collection d'environ 300 modèles en cire, reproduisant très fidèlement autant de sortes de fruits, comprenait notamment 104 variétés de pommes et de poires, 38 variétés de cerises, 35 variétés de prunes et de quetsches, ainsi que 15 variétés de pêches. Un grand nombre de ces fruits en cire remarquables est devenu la propriété de la fondation Wörlitz-Dessau et du musée d'histoire naturelle de Bamberg.

A partir du début du XIXᵉ siècle, le nombre de revues d'horticulture et de culture fruitière augmenta et plusieurs associations et sociétés d'horticulture importantes se créèrent. La Horticultural Society fondée à Londres en 1804 (appelée depuis 1861, la Royal Horticultural Society) a beaucoup contribué au développement de la pomologie. Parmi ses sept membres fondateurs, Sir Joseph Banks (1743–1819), conseiller scientifique compétent, était le directeur non officiel du Royal Botanic Garden de Kew ainsi que le président de la Royal Society de Londres, société des sciences mondialement connue.

A Chiswick, dans les jardins de la Horticultural Society, les chercheurs constituaient des collections de fruits, afin d'éviter à l'avenir toute confusion et méprise dans l'identification des variétés. Ils examinaient les variétés anciennes et nouvelles, provenant de toutes les régions des Iles Britanniques et de l'Europe. Les membres de cette société étaient encouragés à découvrir de nouvelles variétés ou à les cultiver eux-mêmes. Ils étaient également invités à fournir des indications et des recommandations sur les fruits qu'ils connaissaient et sur leur mode de culture, afin qu'il devienne possible d'améliorer la qualité et la variété de l'offre dans les Iles Britanniques.

Un membre fondateur de la Horticultural Society, William Forsyth (1737–1804), jardinier du roi à Kensington, fit paraître, notamment en version allemande, un ouvrage intitulé *Über die Kultur und Behandlung der Obstbäume* (ills. 12 et 13). Un matériel vivant était mis à la disposition des membres ainsi que d'autres sociétés d'horticulture à l'étranger. C'est ainsi que des greffons de variétés de pommes robustes partirent pour les Etats-Unis, dans la vallée de l'Annapolis, pour fonder les bases d'une industrie de la pomme en Nouvelle-Ecosse et au Canada. En 1826, la Royal Horticultural Society a pu fournir, dans le premier *Catalogue of Fruits in the Garden of the Horticultural Society*, les noms exacts de plus de 1200 variétés de pommes, mais dont plus de 400 étaient encore incertains. Cinq ans plus tard, 1396 sortes de fruits étaient répertoriées avec leurs noms précis. Enfin, Thompson publia

tested varieties of apples and pears from the county of Herefordshire, which were used for cider and perry production. Even the finest wine imports were purportedly not as appreciated by the locals of the time as highly as their own products. Between 1813 and 1818 William Hooker published the *Pomona Londinensis* in seven parts, which displayed the best fruits cultivated in British gardens. The 49 hand-painted aquatints, primarily of apples, pears, plums, peaches and nectarines, were supplemented by descriptions written with the assistance of Thomas Knight and members of the Horticultural Society. Hooker completed many more illustrations of fruit varieties on behalf of the Horticultural Society. With great artistic skill he depicted several indigenous varieties as well as a few new dessert varieties from abroad. Hooker was the origin of the humorous motto: "It is better to know apples than some of us."

During the 18th and early 19th centuries many artists and engravers specialized in pomological motifs. Still-life painters produced magnificent pictures and studies of pieces of fruit. This realism arose from a harmony between true pomological interest and artistic ability. Such interest was widespread among amateur artists, a large proportion of whom were women, who were generally barred from enrollment in art academies and therefore privately trained. Detailed manuals by recognized artists on drawing and painting fruits became very popular as a result. Many of these instruction manuals, which were often not comprehensive, illustrated their introductions to the art of drawing and painting with well-made fruit studies. Such paintings were an integral part of the cultural life of the upper-middle class or nobility: they adorned walls, decorated splendid porcelain vessels, tiles and tableware (ills. 14 and 15), were the inspiration for faïence, textiles and even furniture. The crowning glory was the display of fruit both real and artificial on the dessert tables of the aristocracy. All these examples only confirm that during the experimental phase of pomology the different species and varieties were classified mainly by their aesthetic qualities. Artists and pomologists, fruit-growers, art enthusiasts and fruit lovers alike were fascinated by the variety in the shapes, sizes, colours and surface structures of natural fruits, quite apart from the pleasures they offered the palate. The more usual two-dimensional images could be equally impressive.

The illustrations particularly in the splendid pomonas may have been true to nature, but they were valued mostly for their aesthetic appeal. They were masterpieces in which the pomological knowledge of the time was enriched by an aesthetic dimension. Fine artists and pomologists enjoyed a symbiotic relationship: as the latter bred new varieties of fruits by experimentation and horticultural expertise, the former sought to depict and publish the products of their efforts using their own refined skills. The artists, too, experimented in their quest for suitable means to represent the fruits both realistically and aesthetically. Fruit illustrations were avidly collected and discussed by pomologists and art lovers alike. Enchanted musings over these artistically presented objects of research led from wonder and astonishment to studied observation and careful comparison and could ultimately issue forth in the form of rigorous pomological results.

As the number of fruit varieties began to diminish from 1830 onward, there was a corresponding decline in the number of magnificent books on fruits. Illustrations published from then on lack the fascinating individuality which characterized the heyday of pomology.

Uta Pellgrü-Gagel

Fruchtsammlungen angelegt mit dem Ziel, Unklarheiten bzw. Verwechslungen bei der Identifikation von Sorten künftig zu vermeiden. Alte und neue Sorten, die aus allen Teilen der Britischen Inseln sowie aus Europa stammten, wurden untersucht. Die Mitglieder wurden ermutigt, neue Sorten zu suchen oder selbst zu züchten. Andererseits sollten sie Hinweise und Empfehlungen zu Fruchtsorten und deren Anbau geben, damit eine Steigerung der Qualität und des Obstsortiments auf den Britischen Inseln erzielt werden konnte.

Von William Forsyth (1737–1804), königlicher Gärtner in Kensington und Gründungsmitglied der Horticultural Society, erschien auch in deutscher Ausgabe das Werk *Über die Kultur und Behandlung der Obstbäume* (Abb. 12 und 13). Den eigenen Mitgliedern wie auch denen ausländischer Gesellschaften des Gartenbaus wurde lebendes Material zur Verfügung gestellt. So gingen zum Beispiel Edelreiser von robusten Apfelsorten auf die Reise nach Amerika ins Annapolistal, woraufhin sich die neuschottländische und kanadische Apfelindustrie gründete. 1826 konnte Robert Thompson, der Verantwortliche für Früchte innerhalb der Horticultural Society, im ersten *Catalogue of Fruits in the Garden of the Horticultural Society* die richtigen Namen von mehr als 1200 Apfelsorten angeben, wobei bei über 400 Namen die genaue Bezeichnung noch ungewiss war. Fünf Jahre später waren 1396 Apfelsorten mit ihrem präzisen Namen erfasst. Schließlich gab Thompson in Zusammenarbeit mit John Lindley (1799–1865), Mitglied der Horticultural Society und Botanikprofessor am University College in London, das *Pomological Magazine* (1828–1830) mit präzisen Illustrationen heraus. Diese Zeitschrift enthält ausführliche Beschreibungen und Einschätzungen der gebräuchlichsten einheimischen und ausländischen Sorten, die einerseits in Dessert-Obst als pure, frische Kost und andererseits in kulinarisches Obst zur Verarbeitung in Speisen unterteilt sind.

In Zusammenhang mit dem Boom pomologischer Studien ist die Entstehung von luxuriösen Pomonas seit dem Beginn des 19. Jahrhunderts zu sehen. Diese zumeist sehr großformatigen, in kleiner Anzahl herausgegebenen Bücher enthalten einige der bezauberndsten Bilder von Früchten, die jemals geschaffen wurden. Obgleich sie als wissenschaftliches Anschauungsmaterial relevant waren, ist ihre enorme ästhetische Bedeutung hervorzuheben. Sie waren eben nicht Illustrationen, sondern Kunstwerke. Die gegenüber dem Text dominierenden Abbildungen wurden mittels der neuen künstlerischen Techniken Punktiermanier und Aquatinta geschaffen. In Frankreich wurde von 1807 bis 1835 eine vollständig neu bearbeitete Ausgabe von Duhamel du Monceaus *Traité des arbres fruitiers* (1768) unter demselben Titel in Teillieferungen herausgegeben. Die Autoren Pierre-Antoine Poiteau (1766–1854), Botaniker und Leiter der Baumschulen in Versailles, und Pierre Jean François Turpin (1775–1840), Botaniker und Pflanzenphysiologe, erstellten gemeinsam dieses umfangreiche Werk mit künstlerisch hervorragenden Tafeln, beispielsweise zu 108 Birnensorten, 57 Apfel-, 49 Pflaumen- und 29 Kirschsorten.

Im Jahre 1811 – ein Jahr vor der Herausgabe der *Pomona Britannica* von George Brookshaw – erschien die *Pomona Herefordiensis*. Der Verfasser Thomas Andrew Knight (1759–1839), seit 1810 Präsident der Horticultural Society, konnte für die 30 Abbildungen einen seinerzeit bedeutenden englischen pomologischen Illustrator gewinnen: William Hooker (1779–1832). Auf den kolorierten Aquatinten sind vor allem altbewährte Apfel- und Birnensorten aus der Grafschaft Herefordshire abgebildet, die für die Most- und Weinproduktion verwendet wurden. Sogar die edelsten Importweine sollen bei den damaligen Einheimischen nicht so beliebt gewesen sein wie die eigenen Produkte. Von 1813 bis 1818 brachte William Hooker die *Pomona Londinensis* mit den besten in britischen Gärten kultivierten Früchten in sieben Teilen heraus. Den

en collaboration avec John Lindley (1799–1865), membre de la Horticultural Society et professeur de botanique au University College de Londres, le *Pomological Magazine* (1828–1830), illustré à l'aide de dessins précis. Cette revue contenait des descriptions et des évaluations détaillées des espèces locales et étrangères les plus courantes. Ces espèces classées en fruits à dessert se dégustant tels quels, c'est-à-dire nature, et en fruits culinaires, intervenant dans la préparation des plats.

En lien avec ce formidable essor des études pomologiques, de luxueux Pomonas ont vu le jour à partir du début du XIXᵉ siècle. Ces livres, en général de très grand format, publiés en un nombre restreint d'exemplaires, contiennent quelques-unes des plus exquises images de fruits jamais réalisées. Bien que conçus pour servir de matériel scientifique, il convient de souligner leur très grande qualité esthétique. Plus que des illustrations, c'étaient de véritables œuvres d'art. Ces images qui dominent, dans le livre, par rapport au texte, ont été créées au moyen de nouvelles techniques artistiques : la gravure en pointillé et l'aquatinte. En France, une version totalement remaniée du *Traité des arbres fruitiers* de Duhamel du Monceau est publiée entre 1807 et 1835 sous le même titre en une série de volumes. Les auteurs Pierre-Antoine Poiteau (1766–1854), botaniste et directeur de la pépinière de Versailles, et Pierre Jean François Turpin (1775–1840), également botaniste et phytophysiologiste, ont réalisé ensemble cet ouvrage volumineux en y incluant d'admirables planches, très artistiques, reproduisant par exemple 108 variétés de poires, 57 variétés de pommes, 49 variétés de prunes et 29 variétés de cerises.

En 1811, un an avant la sortie de la *Pomona Britannica* de George Brookshaw, paraît le *Pomona Herefordiensis*. Son auteur, Thomas Andrew Knight (1759–1839), président de la Horticultural Society depuis 1810, avait pu associer à son entreprise le grand dessinateur anglais de motifs pomologiques, William Hooker (1779–1832), pour la réalisation des 30 reproductions de son ouvrage. Ces aquatintes coloriées représentent principalement les variétés anciennes de pommes et de poires du comté de Herefordshire. Ces fruits donnaient des cidres et des vins que les gens du pays semblaient préférer aux vins d'importation les plus fins. De 1813 à 1818, William Hooker fait paraître en sept volumes la *Pomona Londinensis*, présentant les meilleurs fruits cultivés dans les jardins britanniques. Les 49 aquatintes coloriées, représentant surtout des variétés de pommes, de poires, de prunes, de pêches et de nectarines, sont complétées par des descriptions de fruits, réalisées avec l'aide de Thomas Knight et d'autres membres de la Horticultural Society. Hooker créa encore beaucoup d'autres dessins de fruits pour le compte de la Horticultural Society. Avec un grand savoir-faire artistique, il reproduisit ainsi de très nombreuses variétés locales ainsi que d'excellentes variétés, récemment reçues de l'étranger. Le dessinateur avait eu ce mot d'humour : « Il est préférable de connaître les pommes que certains d'entre les hommes ».

Au XVIIIᵉ siècle et au début du XIXᵉ, beaucoup de dessinateurs et de graveurs se spécialisèrent dans l'image pomologique. Des peintres de natures mortes réalisaient de magnifiques peintures et études de fruits, dont l'effet réaliste était le reflet d'une grande maîtrise artistique doublé d'un vif intérêt pour la pomologie. Des artistes amateurs, et surtout des femmes – autodidactes, parce que l'accès aux académies leur était généralement fermé – étaient particulièrement demandeuses d'indications précises sur l'art de dessiner et de peindre les fruits. Ainsi, les manuels de dessin publiés par les artistes connurent une large diffusion. Ces ouvrages peu épais pouvaient contenir, outre des indications sur la manière de dessiner et de peindre, de belles illustrations de fruits.

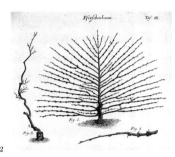

12

Peach tree – Fig. 1: an old hollow peach tree, fig. 2: a branch on a larger scale, fig. 3: a branch of an old peach tree, 1804
William Forsyth, copperplate engraving

Unlike the old, unprofessionally pruned peach branch (fig. 3), Forsyth explains in figure 1 how proper pruning can achieve a high yield of fruits even with older peach trees.

Pfirsichbaum – Fig. 1: Ein alter hohler Pfirsichbaum, Fig. 2: Ein größerer Pfirsichzweig, Fig. 3: Ein alter Pfirsichzweig, 1804
William Forsyth, Kupferstich

Durch den Vergleich mit einem alten, unprofessionell beschnittenen Pfirsichzweig (Fig. 3) erklärt Forsyth anhand von Figur 1, wie durch einen fachmännischen Baumschnitt auch bei einem älteren Pfirsichbaum ein hoher Fruchtertrag erzielt werden kann.

Pêcher – Fig. 1: Vieux pêcher creux, Fig. 2: Grande branche de pêcher, Fig. 3: Branche d'un vieux pêcher, 1804
Gravure sur cuivre de William Forsyth

Par comparaison avec la vieille branche de pêcher, taillée sans savoir-faire professionnel (Fig. 3), Forsyth explique à la figure 1 comment une taille professionnelle peut, même sur un vieux pêcher, donner lieu à une importante production de fruits.

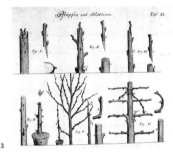

13

Grafting and budding – Methods of propagating cultivars of fruit, 1804
William Forsyth, copperplate engraving

Forsyth introduces, among other things, grafting (figs. I–III): a twig (scion) from a fruit cultivar is united with a robust variety, e.g., a wild version of the same species (understock). Figure IV demonstrates another grafting method by which only the bud (eye) is attached to the understock by means of an appropriate cut under the bark.

Pfropfen und Ablaktieren – Methoden zur Vermehrung kultivierter Obstsorten, 1804
William Forsyth, Kupferstich

Forsyth stellt unter anderem das Pfropfen (Fig. I.–III.) vor: Ein Zweig (Reiser) einer veredelten Obstsorte wird mit einer robusten, zum Beispiel wild wachsenden Obstsorte derselben Art (Unterlage) verbunden. Figur IV. zeigt eine weitere Veredlungsmethode, bei der lediglich ein Triebansatz (Auge) durch einen fachgerechten Schnitt unter die Rinde der Unterlage eingesetzt wird.

Greffe et Ablation – Méthodes pour créer de nouvelles variétés cultivées, 1804
Gravure sur cuivre de William Forsyth

Forsyth présente entre autres la technique de la greffe (Fig. I–III) : une branche (greffon) d'une variété de fruit sélectionnée, est implantée sur une variété robuste, par exemple sauvage (porte-greffe). La figure IV montre une autre méthode de greffage dans laquelle une simple amorce de pousse (œil) est insérée par incision sous l'écorce du porte-greffe, cette intervention nécessitant l'expertise d'un professionnel.

Lidded jar with fruits: Pears, apples, grapes and berries, 2nd half of the 18th century From Delft. *De Porceleyne Claeuw*. Beige earthenware, white glaze. Decorated in the fireproof colors green, violet, ochre, red and blue.

The plasticity of the almost naturally coloured fruits adds to the charm of this jar. The three-dimensional pear-shaped handles, and the bunch of grapes crowning the fruit arrangement as the lid knob, are particularly haptic.

Deckeldose mit Früchten: Birnen, Äpfel, Weintrauben und Beeren, 2. Hälfte 18. Jh.
Aus Delft, *De Porceleyne Claeuw*. Beiger Scherben, weiße Glasur. Dekor in den Scharffeuerfarben Grün, Violett, Ockergelb, Rot und Blau

Ein großes sinnliches Vergnügen stellt sich beim Betrachten dieser Dose mit ihren plastischen Früchten in annähernd natürlichen Farben ein. Der hinzukommende Tastsinn wird durch die in ihrer Dreidimensionalität herausragenden beiden Birnen als Henkel und die das Fruchtarrangement krönenden Weintrauben als Deckelknauf angesprochen.

Boîte décorée de fruits : poires, pommes, raisins et baies, 2ᵉ moitié du XVIIIᵉ siècle
De Delft. *De Porceleyne Claeuw*. Éclats de porcelaine beige, émail blanc. Couleurs résistant au feu : vert, violet, jaune ocre, rouge et bleu

La contemplation de cette boîte, avec ses fruits d'une grande plasticité, peints dans des couleurs quasi naturelles, procure un grand plaisir sensuel. Le sens du toucher est mobilisé par les deux poires en trois dimensions, qui forment les anses, et par les raisins qui couronnent l'arrangement de fruits, et servent ainsi de pommeau, au sommet du couvercle.

China pieces from a set adorned with a cornflower-blue band and painted fruits, flowers and insects, for Elector Friedrich August III of Saxony: tureen, tureen basin, 1777
Johann Eleazar Zeissig, known as Schenau, decorated the porcelain vessels shaped by Michel Victor Acier

The elector of Saxony, who indulged his passion for botanical study during his leisure time, was doubtless delighted with these finely painted fruits.

Teile aus dem Service mit kornblumenblauem Band und Früchte-, Blumen- und Insektenmalerei für Kurfürst Friedrich August III. von Sachsen: Terrine, Terrinenschale, 1777
Johann Eleazar Zeissig, gen. Schenau, dekorierte die von Michel Victor Acier gestalteten Formen aus Porzellan

Der sächsische Kurfürst, der sich in seiner Freizeit liebend gern mit botanischen Studien befasste, war wohl begeistert von dieser filigranen Fruchtmalerei.

Pièces du service au ruban bleu-bleuet, avec peintures de fruits, de fleurs et d'insectes, appartenant au prince électeur Auguste III de Saxe : soupière, plat à soupière, 1777
Johann Eleazar Zeissig, appelé Schenau, décora les formes de porcelaine créées par Michel Victor Acier

Le prince électeur de Saxe, qui aimait, dans ses moments de loisirs, s'adonner à l'étude de la botanique, se délectait de ces peintures de fruits en filigrane.

49 kolorierten Aquatinten, vor allem von Apfel-, Birnen-, Pflaumen-, Pfirsich- und Nektarinensorten, wurden Fruchtbeschreibungen hinzugefügt, die in Assistenz von Thomas Knight und Mitgliedern der Horticultural Society erstellt wurden. Hooker fertigte noch viele Abbildungen von Fruchtsorten im Auftrag der Horticultural Society an. Mit großer künstlerischer Fertigkeit bildete er etliche einheimische wie auch einige der edlen neu eingetroffenen Sorten aus dem Ausland ab. Von Hooker stammt ebenfalls der humorvolle Ausspruch: „Es ist besser, Äpfel zu kennen als einige von uns (Zeitgenossen)."

Im 18. und frühen 19. Jahrhundert gab es viele Zeichner und Stecher, die sich auf pomologische Abbildungen spezialisierten. Stillleben-Maler fertigten herrliche Fruchtbilder und Fruchtstudien an, deren realistische Wirkung sich aus dem harmonischen Einklang von pomologischem Interesse und künstlerischer Fähigkeit ergab. Amateur-Künstler und vor allem privat ausgebildete Frauen, denen der Zugang zu den Kunstakademien in der Regel versperrt blieb, waren besonders interessiert an detaillierten Anweisungen zum Zeichnen und Malen von Früchten. Daher waren die von Künstlern herausgegebenen Zeichenbücher sehr populär. Diese oft nicht umfangreichen Lehrbücher enthielten neben einer Anweisung zum Zeichnen und Malen auch gelungene Frucht-Illustrationen. Abbildungen von Früchten waren ein fester Bestandteil der großbürgerlichen und adligen Kultur: Sie schmückten nicht nur die Wände, sondern zierten auch prächtige Gefäße, Fliesen und Speiseservices aus Porzellan (Abb. 14 und 15) sowie Textilien und Mobiliar. Die Krönung waren die künstlichen und echten Früchte, die auf den herrschaftlichen Dessert-Tafeln präsentiert wurden. Durch all diese Beispiele bestätigt sich umso mehr, dass Fruchtarten und -sorten in der experimentellen Phase der Pomologie vor allem nach ästhetischen Gesichtspunkten klassifiziert wurden. Künstler wie Pomologen und Obstgärtner, Kunstliebhaber wie Obstliebhaber waren fasziniert von den variierenden Größen, Formen, Farben und Oberflächenstrukturen der natürlichen Früchte, ganz abgesehen vom Genuss, der beim Verzehr empfunden werden konnte. Ebenso beeindruckend konnten die zumeist zweidimensionalen Abbilder der Früchte erscheinen.

Die Abbildungen, vor allem in den prächtigen Pomonas, mögen noch so naturgetreu gewesen sein, geschätzt wurden sie vor allem auf Grund ihrer ästhetischen Wirkung. Sie sind Kunstwerke, in denen das pomologische Wissen der damaligen Zeit um die Dimension des Ästhetischen erweitert wurde. Die bildenden Künstler und Pomologen standen in einem symbiotischen Verhältnis zueinander: So wie Letztere durch das Experimentieren und mit ihren gärtnerischen Fähigkeiten neue Obstsorten kreierten, wollten erstere mit ihren künstlerischen Fähigkeiten diese Züchtungsergebnisse abbilden und veröffentlichen. Auch die Künstler experimentierten insofern, wie sie die passenden künstlerischen Mittel finden mussten, um die Früchte realistisch und zugleich ästhetisch darzustellen. Leidenschaftlich und begeistert wurden Abbildungen mit Früchten von Pomologen und Kunstliebhabern gesammelt und diskutiert. Das entzückte Verweilen vor den ästhetisch abgebildeten Forschungsgegenständen führte über das Sichwundern und Staunen hinaus zum bewussten Betrachten und Vergleichen und konnte in pomologischen Erkenntnissen manifestiert werden.

Seit 1830 ist zunehmend ein Rückgang der prächtigen Früchtebücher wie auch der Obstsortenanzahl zu verzeichnen. Den nachfolgend bis in die jüngste Zeit veröffentlichten Abbildungen fehlt oft jene individuelle Note, die beim Betrachten der älteren Abbildungen aus der Blütezeit der Pomologie so sehr faszinieren kann.

Uta Pellgrü-Gagel

Les représentations de fruits faisaient partie de la culture bourgeoise et aristocratique de l'époque. Elles ornaient superbement les murs, certains récipients, les carrelages, les services de porcelaine (ill. 14 et 15), les textiles et les meubles. Cet art culminait dans la présentation de fruits naturels et artificiels sur les tables à dessert des grandes maisons bourgeoises et aristocratiques. Tous ces exemples expliquent d'autant mieux pourquoi, dans la phase expérimentale de la pomologie, les espèces et les variétés de fruits étaient surtout classées selon des points de vue esthétiques. Les artistes, mais aussi les pomologues, les cultivateurs de fruits, les amateurs d'art et les amateurs de fruits étaient fascinés par la grande variété de tailles, de formes, de couleurs, de structure superficielle des fruits naturels, sans parler du plaisir que procurait leur dégustation. Les reproductions de fruits, généralement bidimensionnelles, pouvaient tout autant impressionner. Malgré la fidélité de leur rendu dans les magnifiques *Pomonas*, elles étaient surtout appréciées pour leur effet esthétique et constituaient des œuvres d'art, dans lesquelles le savoir pomologique de l'époque s'enrichissait d'une dimension esthétique. Les artistes et les pomologues travaillaient en symbiose. Alors que les uns créaient de nouvelles sortes de fruits en expérimentant et en appliquant leur savoir-faire horticole, les autres appliquaient toute leur habileté artistique à reproduire et à publier les résultats de ces recherches. D'ailleurs, les artistes expérimentaient eux aussi, dans la mesure où ils devaient trouver des moyens techniques adéquats pour représenter les fruits à la fois avec art et réalisme.

Les illustrations des artistes étaient ensuite collectionnées avec passion et commentées avec enthousiasme par les pomologues et les amateurs d'art. Le ravissement avec lequel le spectateur attentif contemplait ces objets de la recherche pomologique, pouvait au-delà du stade du pur émerveillement, l'amener à une démarche d'observation et de comparaison, qui le conduisait à acquérir à son tour un savoir pomologique.

A partir de 1830, on assiste à un déclin de ces somptueux livres sur les fruits et parallèlement, à une diminution du nombre de variétés. Aux reproductions publiées depuis cette date jusqu'à aujourd'hui, il manque souvent cette note personnelle qui fascine tant à la contemplation des illustrations plus anciennes, réalisées à l'époque du plein épanouissement de la pomologie.

Uta Pellgrü-Gagel

CATALOGUE OF PLATES
Katalog der Tafeln | Catalogue des planches

Of the originally anticipated 93 plates from the *Pomona Britannica* only 90 have been included here. The numbering of the plates in the present catalogue conforms to that of the original publication, the two exceptions being plates 19 and 20, which have been reallocated to the species to which they belong. The names of the varieties in the legends refer to the fruits on the plates in order from top left to bottom right. Missing varieties or those that could not be classified are indicated by a dash. The selected recipes have been taken from the historic cookery book *Universal-Lexikon der Kochkunst* (Universal Lexicon of the Culinary Art, 1890).

Von den ursprünglich vorgesehenen 93 Tafeln der *Pomona Britannica* wurden nur 90 ausgeführt. Der folgende Katalog übernimmt Brookshaws englische Früchtenamen und folgt in der Nummerierung der abgebildeten Tafeln durchgängig dem Original, lediglich die Abfolge der Tafeln 19 und 20 wurde er Gruppierung der Arten angepasst. Die Sortennamen in den Legenden richten sich nach der Abfolge der Früchte auf den Tafeln von links oben nach rechts unten. Fehlende oder nicht bestimmbare Sorten werden mit einem Gedankenstrich angezeigt. Die eingefügten Rezepte wurden dem historischen Kochbuch *Universal-Lexikon der Kochkunst* (1890) entnommen.

Sur les 93 planches prévues à l'origine de la *Pomona Britannica*, 90 seulement ont été réalisées. Ce catalogue suit la numérotation des planches illustrées conformément à l'original, sauf exception pour les planches 19 et 20 qui ont été regroupées sous les espèces auxquelles elles appartiennent. Dans les légendes, les noms des variétés se rapportent aux fruits illustrés sur les planches, de haut en bas et de gauche à droite. Les variétés manquantes ou indéterminées sont indiquées par un tiret. Les recettes de cuisine sélectionnées sont issues du livre de cuisine historique *Universal-Lexikon der Kochkunst* (1890).

STRAWBERRIES
Erdbeeren | Fraises

Although the botanical genus *Fragaria* seems to be relatively prevalent, actually only two species of strawberries played a lastingly significant role in its cultivation: the Chilean Beach Strawberry, *Fragaria chiloensis*, and the Meadow Strawberry, *Fragaria virginiana*. A cross between the two species led to our current garden hybrids. The Latin names reveal the American origins of the plants and consequently their relatively late arrival in European fruit baskets. Previously, wild relatives were commonly cultivated in Europe, whose deficiency in size was more than compensated by aromatic flavour. Runnerless plants were being tended in gardens from the 14th century and as early as the 16th century white and yellow-fleshed varieties were being displayed. The everbearing alpine varieties with their multiple blossomings had advantages over the wild varieties, which produce fruit only once annually, but they only became more generally available in the 18th century. The Hautbois Strawberry, *Fragaria moschata*, also played a role in central European horticulture but its dioecious, or bisexual structure, complicated its cultivation.

All these traditional species were largely supplanted by the two American imports. They were initially grown with mixed success in European gardens until a cross between the small-fruited but aromatic, productive and hardy Meadow Strawberry and the firm-fleshed, sweet and somewhat lighter Chilean giant strawberry eventually led to the breakthrough in efforts to breed an economically viable product. The characteristic flavour of this stately fruit led some to equate it with the pineapple, hence its German name *Ananas-Erdbeere*. It became the stock of practically all later varieties, of which many hundreds were known already by the first half the 19th century. Although some of the cheaper mass-produced strawberries today rather make one think back longingly to the fragrantly flavourful traditional varieties, the "queen of strawberries" still crowns our tables, on cakes, as jam, and even as ice-cream, wine and champagne, not to forget the simple fresh fruit with an enticing dollop of whipped cream.

PLATE I

Early Scarlet Strawberry · Late Scarlet · Golden Drop · Pine
Frühe Scharlachrote Erdbeere · Späte Scharlachrote Erdbeere · Golden Drop · Ananas-Erdbeere
Ecarlate précoce · Ecarlate tardive · Golden Drop · Fraise d'ananas

PLATE I.
Painted & Published as the Act directs by the Author G. Brookshaw. March 1805

Obwohl sich die botanische Gattung *Fragaria*, Erdbeere, relativ umfangreich präsentiert, spielten eigentlich nur zwei Arten eine nachhaltig tragende Rolle: die Chile-Erdbeere, *Fragaria chiloensis*, und die Scharlacherdbeere, *Fragaria virginiana*, denn ihre Kreuzung führte zu unseren heutigen Gartenerdbeeren. Die lateinischen Namen verraten bereits die amerikanische Herkunft der Pflanzen und damit wird klar, dass die verlockenden Früchte erst relativ spät die europäische Fruchtpalette bereicherten. Dort wurden sie bis dahin durch ihre wild wachsende Schwester, die Walderdbeere, vertreten, deren volles Aroma immerhin aufwiegen kann, was den Früchten an Größe fehlt. Die ausläuferlosen Pflanzen werden seit dem 14. Jahrhundert in den Gärten kultiviert und im 16. Jahrhundert können auch schon weiß- und gelbfruchtige Sorten bestaunt werden. Die alpine Monatserdbeere bot gegenüber der nur einmal im Jahr tragenden Walderdbeere zwar den Vorteil mehrfacher Blüte und Frucht, doch wurde sie erst im 18. Jahrhundert im größeren Umfang verfügbar. Eine gewisse Rolle im Gartenbau spielte auch die Moschus-Erdbeere (*Fragaria moschata*), die allerdings wegen ihrer Zweihäusigkeit schwieriger zu kultivieren ist.

Alle diese überkommenen Arten wurden jedoch durch die Einfuhr der beiden amerikanischen Arten weitgehend verdrängt. Anfangs in den europäischen Gärten noch mit wechselndem Erfolg gezogen, brachte die Kreuzung der kleinfruchtigen, aber aromatischen, tragfreudigen und winterfesten Scharlacherdbeere mit der festfleischigen, süßen und etwas helleren chilenischen Riesen-Erdbeere schließlich den züchterischen und wirtschaftlichen Durchbruch. Wegen ihres charakteristischen Aromas erhielten die stattlichen Früchte den Namen „Ananas-Erdbeere". Sie wurden zur Urform praktisch aller späteren Züchtungen, von denen bereits in der ersten Hälfte des 19. Jahrhunderts mehrere hundert bekannt waren. Wenn auch manche der heute für den billigen Massenabsatz produzierten Erdbeeren eher sehnsüchtige Gedanken an das volle Aroma früherer, traditionell angebauter Sorten aufkommen lassen, erfreut sich die „Königin der Beeren" einer ungebrochenen Beliebtheit vom Kuchenbelag über die Marmelade bis hin zum Eis und zu Wein und Sekt, nicht zu vergessen die rohen Früchte, veredelt mit einem verlockenden Sahnehäubchen.

PLATE II

Hautboy Strawberry · Chili-Strawberry (Pine Strawberry) · Alpine Red Strawberry · Scarlet Flesh Strawberry
Hautboy-Erdbeere · Riesen- oder Chile-Erdbeere · Scharlachrote Alpen-Erdbeere · Erdbeere mit scharlachrotem Fleisch
Fraise Hautboy · Fraise du Chili (Fraise d'ananas) · Ecarlate alpine · Fraise à chair écarlate

PLATE II.

Painted & Published as the Act directs by the Author G. Brookshaw. March 1804.

Bien que le genre *fragaria* (fraise) soit assez diversement représenté, seules deux espèces ont joué un rôle durable : la fraise du Chili, *fragaria chiloensis*, et la fraise écarlate, *fragaria virginiana*, car leurs croisements ont conduit à nos fraises de jardin d'aujourd'hui. L'origine américaine de ces deux espèces, que nous révèlent leurs noms latins, explique que ce fruit tentant ne soit venu enrichir qu'assez tardivement la palette européenne. En Europe, la fraise n'était connue jusque-là que par sa sœur sauvage, la fraise des bois, dont l'arôme puissant compense une taille très réduite. Plantes sans coulant, c'est-à-dire sans rejetons, les fraises sont cultivées dans les jardins depuis le XIVe siècle. Au XVIe siècle on pouvait déjà admirer des fraises de couleur blanche ou jaune. La variété alpine dite des quatre saisons offrait, par rapport à sa sœur des bois, l'avantage de fructifier plusieurs fois par an, mais ne se cultiva à plus grande échelle qu'à partir du XVIIIe siècle. La fraise capron (*fragaria moschata*) joua elle aussi un certain rôle en horticulture, mais était plus difficile à cultiver à cause de son caractère dioïque.

Toutes ces espèces traditionnelles furent largement supplantées par l'arrivée des deux américaines. En effet, le croisement entre la fraise écarlate, aromatique, de petite taille, mais très productive et résistante au froid hivernal, et la fraise géante du Chili, à chair ferme, sucrée et un peu plus claire, donna des fruits dont la culture connut tout d'abord un succès variable dans les jardins mais qui réussirent finalement à s'imposer sur les marchés et chez les cultivateurs. En raison de leur arôme caractéristique, ces variétés de belle apparence furent appelées « fraises ananas », et devinrent la source de pratiquement toutes les autres développées par la suite, dont on dénombrait plusieurs centaines dès la première moitié du XIXe siècle. Même si les fraises produites aujourd'hui pour une diffusion massive et bon marché éveillent parfois la nostalgie du riche arôme des variétés d'antan, la « reine des fruits rouges » n'a jamais cessé de plaire en donnant lieu aux préparations culinaires les plus variées, depuis les tartes et les confitures jusqu'aux glaces, vins et champagnes, sans oublier le fruit nature, couronné d'une collerette de chantilly.

PLATE III

New Early Prolific (Scarlet Strawberry) · Wood Strawberry · White Alpine
Frühe Fruchtbare Scharlachrote Erdbeere · Walderdbeere · Weiße Alpen-Erdbeere
Fertile hâtive · Fraise des bois · Alpine blanche

RASPBERRIES
Himbeeren | Framboises

The German name, *Himbeere* (formerly *hintber*), for this native of Asia derives from the word hind or doe. We do not know what inspired this name but perhaps these animals and their young savoured the exquisite berries as much as our human forebears. In the strictly botanical sense these are not individual berries, as their name would lead us to think, but an aggregate fruit formed of multiple little hairy drupes that are connected together and easily come off their conical base as a single unit. So the actual edible part of the raspberry when picked is a hollow cup shape. When fresh the fruit dissolves on the tongue with an overwhelming aromatic tang that does not lose its vitality when prepared as jam, dessert or ice-cream, or even as vinegar, syrup, wine or liqueur. This distinctive taste naturally prompted cultivators to try out variations. The resulting hybrids from crosses with species of blackberries, such as the Loganberry (1881) and Black Boysenberry (around 1920), have since managed to gain a considerable share of the market.

Nach der Hirschkuh, der Hinde, wurde die in Asien beheimatete Himbeere benannt, die früher „hintber" hieß. Was den Anlass zu diesem Namen gab, wissen wir nicht, aber vielleicht erfreuten sich die Tiere mit ihren Jungen ebenso am exquisiten Aroma der Früchte, wie auch der Mensch dies seit langem tut. Im streng botanischen Sinn handelt es sich allerdings nicht um eine einzelne Beere, wie der Name vorgaukelt, sondern um eine Sammelfrucht aus lauter kleinen, haarigen Steinfrüchtchen, die zusammenhängen und sich als Ganzes leicht vom zapfenartigen Fruchtboden lösen, so dass als eigentliche, das heißt essbare Himbeere ein hohler Becher übrig bleibt. Frisch genossen entfaltet er, auf der Zunge zergehend, ein überwältigendes Aroma, das die Früchte aber auch verschwenderisch an Zubereitungen weitergeben, von der Marmelade über Süßspeisen bis hin zum Eis, zum Himbeeressig, -sirup, -wein und -wasser. Natürlich reizte ein solches Geschmackserlebnis die Züchter zu dem Versuch, es zu variieren, und so entstanden durch Kreuzung mit Brombeerarten zum Beispiel die Loganbeere (1881) und die schwarze Boysenbeere (um 1920), die sich seither zumindest Teilmärkte erobern konnten.

Originaire d'Asie, la framboise est nommée en allemand d'après la biche, *Hinde*, qui a donné *hintber* puis « Himbeere ». En français, framboise vient de *brambasia*, qui veut dire « mûre » ou d'un mot du XIIᵉ siècle, « frambaise », qui a pu donner « fraise ». Pourquoi dériver ce mot de la biche dans la langue allemande ? Nous ne le savons pas. Peut-être ces animaux et leurs petits se régalaient-ils tout autant que nous de ces baies exquises. A strictement parler, la framboise n'est toutefois pas une simple baie mais un fruit composé d'une multitude de minuscules baies velues, à pépins, qui, ensemble, se détachent facilement du fond conique, pour constituer la partie comestible du fruit, en forme de godet. Quand elle fond sur la langue, la framboise fraîche dégage un arôme pénétrant, qui se transmet généreusement à toutes les préparations réalisées à partir de ce fruit : confitures, desserts, glaces, vinaigres, sirops, alcools et eaux-de-vie. Les cultivateurs ont évidemment tenté de trouver de multiples variantes à cette riche saveur et ont ainsi créé, par croisement avec des variétés de mûres, par exemple la *Loganberry* (ronce-framboise) (1881) et la boysenberry noire (vers 1920) qui, depuis, ont su conquérir certains marchés.

PLATE IV

White Antwerp Raspberry · Red Antwerp Raspberry
Weiße Antwerpener Himbeere · Rote Antwerpener Himbeere
Framboise d'Anvers à gros fruit blanc allongé · Framboise d'Anvers à gros fruit rouge allongé

PLATE IV
Painted & Published as the Act directs by the Author G. Brookshaw. March 1812

CURRANTS

Johannisbeeren | Groseilles · Cassis

John the Baptist is the patron saint of this fruit because it ripens around his feast day, on June 24th. Evidence in our gardens of the currant dates back to the 15th century. The red or yellowish-white berries, formed from their racemes, have been popular ever since for their refreshing sour taste. Blackcurrants differ from their sister varieties not only in flavour but particularly in their content of vitamin C, which is as much as five times higher. Currants are classified among the botanical family *Saxifragaceae*. Being indigenous to northern Europe and America, they were unknown to the Ancient Greeks. The term widely used in southern Germany and Austria for the berries and their related delicious recipes, *Ribisel*, derives from their Latin designation *ribes* – after the name of a sour-tasting species of rhubarb.

Johannes der Täufer fungiert bei ihr als Pate, weil ihre Früchte um den 24. Juni, den Johannitag, reif werden. Seit dem 15. Jahrhundert ist die Johannisbeere in unseren Gärten nachweisbar und seitdem sind die aus den Blütentrauben entstehenden roten oder gelblich-weißen Beeren wegen ihres erfrischend sauren Geschmacks beliebt. Daneben gibt es auch die Schwarze Johannisbeere, die sich nicht nur im Geschmack von ihren Schwestern unterscheidet, sondern insbesondere durch ihren etwa fünfmal höheren Vitamin-C-Gehalt. Botanisch gehört die Johannisbeere zu den Steinbrechgewächsen (*Saxifragaceae*). Sie ist im Norden Europas und Amerikas beheimatet und war deshalb in der Antike unbekannt. Von ihrem lateinischen Namen *ribes* – nach der Bezeichnung einer sauer schmeckenden Rhabarberart – leitet sich auch das in Süddeutschland und Österreich verbreitete „Ribisel" für die Beeren und daraus hergestellte leckere Zubereitungen ab.

Appelée en allemand la «baie de Jean» parce que ses fruits mûrissent vers le 24 juin, jour de la Saint-Jean, la groseille est attestée dans nos jardins depuis le XVe siècle et les baies jaune-blanc ou rouges qui naissent de ses grappes de fleurs ont toujours été appréciées à cause de leur acidité rafraîchissante. Son frère noir, le cassis, se distingue non seulement par son goût mais aussi par une teneur cinq fois plus forte en vitamine C. Dans la classification botanique, la groseille fait partie des saxifragacées. Provenant du nord de l'Europe et d'Amérique, ce fruit était inconnu dans l'Antiquité à cause de ses origines. De son nom latin *ribes*, qui désigne une variété acide de rhubarbe, découle aussi le terme de «Ribisel», répandu au sud de l'Allemagne et en Autriche pour désigner les groseilles et les délicieuses spécialités à base de ce fruit.

PLATE V

Black Currant · White Currant · Dutch Red Currant
Schwarze Johannisbeere · Englische weiße Johannisbeere · Holländische rote Johannisbeere
Cassis · Groseille d'Angleterre à fruit blanc · Groseille de Hollande à fruit rouge

GOOSEBERRIES
Stachelbeeren | Groseilles à maquereau

The 13th-century French poet Rutebeuf was probably the first to mention gooseberries, *Ribes uva-crispa* L., and to record them as *groiselles*. The earliest known illustration dates from two hundred years later, though, as a marginal sketch not in the botanical literature but in a prayer book, the *Breviarium Grimani*, which appeared around 1510–1520. Three decades elapsed before gooseberries were also featured in herbals, first in that of Leonhard Fuchs (1543), even though cultivars were evidently already being grown in many gardens. These unassuming berries all originate from wild varieties native to Europe and Asia, which were selectively cultivated from the 15th century onward to improve their size and flavour. The greatest advances were made in the 18th century, however, in England, where they were successfully crossed with North American species in 1705. By the end of that century some 100 different varieties were known – Brookshaw even speaks of more than 1000 – with white, yellow, green or red berries that were often covered in prickly hairs. Depending on the type and degree of ripeness, these plump fruits range from sour to very sweet and find correspondingly multifarious uses in the kitchen: preserved as spicy chutneys for goose or fish dishes or as jam or stewed fruit – if, that is, they are not consumed fresh.

Der im 13. Jahrhundert lebende französische Dichter Rutebeuf war wohl der Erste, der die Stachelbeere, *Ribes uva-crispa* L., erwähnte und ihr den Namen „groiselle" gab. Zweihundert Jahre später findet sich die früheste bekannte Abbildung, aber nicht in der botanischen Literatur, sondern als Randzeichnung in einem Gebetbuch, dem um 1510–1520 entstandenen *Breviarium Grimani*. Erst drei Jahrzehnte später erscheint die Stachelbeere auch in den Kräuterbüchern, erstmals bei Leonhart Fuchs (1543), obwohl damals Zuchtformen offenbar schon in vielen Gärten anzutreffen waren. Sie stammten alle von der in Europa und Asien einheimischen Wildform ab, die seit dem 15. Jahrhundert zur Verbesserung der Größe und des Geschmacks ihrer unscheinbaren Beeren kultiviert wurde. Der große Durchbruch wurde aber erst im 18. Jahrhundert in England erzielt, wo man seit 1705 nordamerikanische Stachelbeer-Sorten erfolgreich einkreuzte, so dass am Ende des Jahrhunderts bereits etwa hundert verschiedene Sorten – Brookshaw spricht sogar von über tausend – mit weißen, gelben, grünen oder roten, teils borstig behaarten Beeren bekannt waren. Je nach Sorte und Reifegrad variiert deren Geschmack zwischen sauer und sehr süß und dementsprechend vielseitig werden die prallen Früchte auch in der Küche verwendet: in würzigen Chutneys ebenso wie zu Gans oder Fisch, aber auch als Marmelade, Kompott oder roh genossen finden sie dankbare Genießer.

Le poète français du XIIIᵉ siècle, Rutebeuf, a sans doute été le premier à mentionner la groseille à maquereau, ou *ribes uva-crispa* L., qu'il appelait «groiselle». Deux cents ans plus tard, on en trouve la première illustration connue, non pas dans un ouvrage de botanique mais dans un livre de prière, le *Breviarium Grimani*, écrit vers 1510–1520. Il faut attendre encore trente ans avant que la groseille à maquereau ne fasse son entrée dans les livres d'herboristerie, le premier étant celui de Leonhart Fuchs (1543), bien qu'à l'époque, on trouvait déjà des formes cultivées dans nombre de jardins. Elles provenaient toutes d'une même variété qui poussait à l'état sauvage en Europe et en Asie et qui fut cultivée à partir du XVᵉ siècle pour améliorer la taille et le goût de ces baies de peu d'apparence. Mais la grande percée de la groseille à maquereau date du XVIIIᵉ siècle, en Angleterre, depuis qu'on la croisa, à partir de 1705, avec sa sœur américaine pour obtenir, dès la fin du siècle, une centaine de sortes nouvelles – plus de mille d'après Brookshaw – aux baies blanches, jaunes, vertes ou rouges, et au duvet parfois rêche. Selon la variété et le degré de maturité, le goût passe de l'acide au très sucré, donnant lieu aux recettes les plus diverses. Incorporée à des chutneys épicés, accompagnant un rôti d'oie ou un plat de poisson, préparée sous forme de confiture ou de compote, ou dégustée fraîche, elle mérite toujours la reconnaissance des gourmets.

PLATE VI

Early Green Hairy · Child's Golden Lion · Alcock's Duke of York · Lomaxe's Victory · Mill's Champion · Warrington Red · Mill's Langley Green · Eden's Elibore · Hill's Sir Peter Teazle · Woodwards White-Smith · Tillotson's Seedling · Warwickshire Conqueror · Rawlinson's Duke of Bridgewater · Clyton's Britania · Hall's Porcupine · Arrowsmith's Ruler of England · Fox's Jolly Smoker

Frühe Grüne Stachelbeere · Wunderbare Rauchbeere · Lomaxe's Victory · Mill's Champion · Unvergleichliche Rauchbeere · Mills Grüne · Eden's Elibore · Hill's Sir Peter Teazle · Feinriechende Zungenbeere · Tillotsons Sämling · Eroberer von Warwickshire · Rawlinson's Duke of Bridgewater · Spätreifende Wendelbeere · Hall's Porcupine · Arrowsmith's Ruler of England · Fox's Jolly Smoker

Green Gascoigne · — · Alcock's Duke of York · Victoire · Mill's Champion · Warrington Red · Mill's Langley Green · Eden's Elibore · — · White-Smith · — · — · Rawlinson's Duke of Bridgewater · Clyton's Britania · Hall's Porcupine · Arrowsmith's Ruler of England · Fox's Jolly Smoker

PLATE VI.
Printed & Published as the Act directs by the Author G.Brookshaw July 1st 1805.

CHERRIES
Kirschen | Cerises

If we are to believe Pliny, then it was Lucullus who brought cherries to Rome in 64 B.C. from Cerasus on the Black Sea, now known as Giresun in Turkey. But it remains unclear whether a particularly tasty cultivar of the Sweet Cherry native to Europe, *Prunus avium*, was involved or the Sour Cherry, *Prunus cerasus*, which is prevalent throughout Asia Minor. The two varieties have only been clearly distinguished since the early 19th century and are botanically closely related to plums, peaches and apricots. In any event the wild varieties were a part of human life at least since the Stone Age, as is evidenced by cherry-stone finds among settlement remains.

The Greeks also appreciated cherries and already knew about the medicinal qualities of the gum exuded by the tree when gashed, and they probably also cultivated them in their colonies. The Romans did likewise and just 120 years after Lucullus early cultivars of cherries were growing throughout central Europe and as far as Britain. By the mid-16th century about 15 different varieties were known; today that figure has risen to many hundreds. From the sour *Glaskirsche*, crossbred in the 17th century from sweet and sour cherries, the Hard-Fleshed Cherry was developed which still dominates the market today alongside the softer Heart Cherry. One particular variety of sour cherry, the Marasca, formerly native to the Balkans, is used to produce maraschino liqueur. Otherwise, Sour Cherries are very suitable as stews or preserves, but are also well liked in the form of juice or jam. Cherry schnaps, or *Kirschwasser*, is made from Sweet Cherries with some wild varieties for added flavor.

One should caution against combining cherries with plain water, though, since a drink after a generous helping of cherries causes the pectin in the fruit to swell and may cause unpleasant stomach pains and indigestion. An old German saying also questions the wisdom of eating cherries in the company of powerful lords because they would spit the pits into the faces of those sitting opposite them. Such uncouthness ought to have become rare these days, but if one must make use of the stones, which are poisonous when bitten into, then a cherry-stone pack is advised, which as a prewarmed compress can alleviate many an ailment.

PLATE VII

May-Duke · White-Heart Cherry · Black-Heart Cherry
Rote Maikirsche · Weiße Herzkirsche (Frühe Bernsteinkirsche) · Gemeine Schwarze Herzkirsche
Royale hâtive · Cerise cœur blanc · Guigne noire (Guigne à gros fruits noir)

PLATE VII
Painted and Published as the Act directs by the Author C. Brookshaw May 1803.

Glauben wir Plinius, dann war es Lukullus, der 64 v. Chr. aus Cerasunt am Schwarzen Meer, dem heutigen Giresun in der Türkei, die Kirschen nach Rom brachte. Es bleibt aber unklar, ob es sich dabei um eine besonders wohlschmeckende Zuchtsorte der in Europa heimischen Süßkirsche, *Prunus avium*, oder aber der in Kleinasien verbreiteten Sauerkirsche, *Prunus cerasus*, handelte. Beide Sorten wurden erst seit dem frühen 19. Jahrhundert klar unterschieden und sind botanisch eng mit Pflaume, Pfirsich und Aprikose verwandt. Jedenfalls begleiteten Wildformen der roten Früchte den Menschen mindestens schon seit der Steinzeit, wie Funde von Kirschkernen in Siedlungsresten belegen.

Die Griechen schätzten Kirschen ebenfalls, kannten auch schon das medizinisch genutzte Gummi, das der Baum bei Verletzungen ausscheidet, und brachten den Anbau wohl auch in ihre Kolonien. Ähnlich verhielten sich die Römer und nur 120 Jahre nach Lukullus wuchsen frühe Kulturformen der Kirsche bereits in ganz Mitteleuropa bis nach Britannien. In der Mitte des 16. Jahrhunderts kennt man etwa 15 verschiedene Sorten, heute sind es viele hundert. Über die im 17. Jahrhundert durch Kreuzung von Süß- und Sauerkirsche gezüchtete Glaskirsche wurden die festfleischigere Knorpelkirschen gezüchtet, die sich noch heute neben den weicheren Herzkirschen auf dem Markt behaupten. Ehemals auf dem Balkan heimisch war auch eine besondere Varietät der Sauerkirschen, die Maraska-Kirsche, aus der der Maraschino-Likör hergestellt wird. Ansonsten eignen sich Sauerkirschen sehr gut als Einmach- oder Konservenobst, sind aber auch als Saft oder Marmelade nach wie vor beliebt. Zum Brennen des alkoholischen Kirschwassers werden Süßkirschen, teilweise auch die aromatischen Früchte von Wildarten, verwendet.

Ansonsten ist die Verbindung von Kirschen und Wasser mit Vorsicht zu genießen, denn nach dem ausgiebigen Genuss von Kirschen bringt getrunkenes Wasser das in den Früchten enthaltene Pektin zum Quellen und kann dadurch unangenehme Magen- und Verdauungsbeschwerden auslösen. Zur Vorsicht mahnt auch ein altes deutsches Sprichwort, das behauptet, mit großen Herren sei schlecht Kirschen essen, weil sie ihrem Gegenüber die Kerne ins Gesicht spuckten. Diese Unart dürfte heute selten geworden sein, aber wenn man die beim Zerbeißen giftigen Steine unbedingt nutzen möchte, dann bietet sich ein Kirschkernsäckchen an, das als vorgewärmte Auflage bei manchen Beschwerden helfen kann.

PLATE VIII

Early-May · Adam's Crown · Red-Heart Cherry
Frühe Mai-Herzkirsche · Adams Herzkirsche · Rote Herzkirsche
Guigne précoce · Guigne d'Adam · Guigne rouge

PLATE VIII
Painted & Published as the Act directs by the Author G. Brookshaw, 1807

A en croire Pline, ce fut Lucullus qui, en 64 av. J.-C., rapporta la cerise à Rome. Il l'avait découverte à Cérasonte sur la mer Noire, aujourd'hui Giresun en Turquie. Toutefois, nous ignorons s'il s'agissait d'une variété cultivée, particulièrement savoureuse, de la cerise douce, originaire d'Europe, appelée *prunus avium*, ou de la griotte acide (*prunus cerasus*), très répandue en Asie mineure. Les deux sortes n'ont été clairement distinguées qu'au début du XIXe siècle et sont étroitement apparentées à la prune, à la pêche et à l'abricot. Des formes sauvages de ces fruits rouges étaient déjà connues à l'âge de pierre, comme en témoignent des noyaux de cerise trouvés dans des vestiges d'anciens sites habités.

Les Grecs ont eux aussi apprécié la cerise et connaissaient la gomme qui suinte des blessures de l'arbre, puisqu'ils l'utilisaient à des fins médicinales. Sans doute ont-ils aussi implanté le cerisier dans leurs colonies. Les Romains ont fait de même, et 120 ans après l'initiative de Lucullus, des variétés précoces de cerise cultivée poussaient dans toute l'Europe centrale jusqu'en Grande-Bretagne. Au milieu du XVIe siècle, on en connaissait environ 15 sortes différentes et aujourd'hui plusieurs centaines. Par croisement entre cerises douces et acides, on obtint, au cours du XVIIe siècle, la griotte de culture, qui à son tour donna naissance au bigarreau, à chair ferme, encore bien présent aujourd'hui sur le marché, et à la guigne, plus tendre. Une variété particulière de cerise acide, la marasque, originaire des Balkans, parfume la liqueur appelée marasquin. Les cerises acides se prêtent aussi très bien à la confection de conserves, et sont également appréciées en jus ou en confiture. Pour la distillation du kirsch (eau-de-vie de cerise), on utilise des cerises douces, ou parfois le fruit aromatique de certaines variétés sauvages.

En général, la combinaison de l'eau et de la cerise demande une certaine prudence, car l'eau bue après une dégustation de cerises fait gonfler la pectine contenue dans les fruits et peut occasionner des désagréments gastriques et digestifs. Un vieux dicton allemand enseigne également la prudence quand on mange des cerises avec de grands messieurs, qui n'hésitent pas à cracher leurs noyaux à la figure de leur vis-à-vis – une inconvenance heureusement fort rare de nos jours. Mais si l'on tient absolument à utiliser ces noyaux, qui sont toxiques quand on mord dedans, on peut les réunir dans un petit sac qu'on appliquera chaud sur le corps en cas de troubles.

PLATE IX

Bleeding Heart · Ox-Heart · Maple-Heart
Blut-Herzkirsche · Ochsenherzkirsche · Maple-Heart
Guigne sanguinole · Guigne des bœufs · Guigne d'érable

PLATE IX.

Painted & Published as the Act directs by the Author G. Brookshaw July 1.1805.

CHERRY PUDDING WITH SEMOLINA

1 quart milk, medium grain semolina, 10 oz butter, 10–12 eggs, 4 1/2 oz ground almonds,
5 1/2 oz sugar, grated rind of 1 lemon, 2 teaspoonsful of ground cinnamon, 2 lb pitted sour cherries

Stir enough medium grain semolina into one quart of simmering milk to make a thick gruel, keep it stirring until smooth to prevent lumps; then pour it out and allow it to cool. Next beat ten ounces of butter until creamy and gradually add the yolks of ten to twelve eggs, four and a half ounces of ground almonds, two and a third ounces of sugar, the grated rind of one lemon, two teaspoonsful of ground cinnamon, the gruel, the stiffly beaten whites of ten eggs and two pounds of pitted sour cherries; pour it all into a buttered baking pan and bake the pudding for a good hour at moderate heat.

KIRSCH‑PUDDING MIT GRIES

1 Liter Milch, mittelfeiner Gries, 250 Gramm Butter, 10–12 Eier, 125 Gramm gestoßene Mandeln,
160 Gramm Zucker, abgeriebene Schale einer Zitrone, 2 Kaffeelöffel gestoßenen Zimmt,
1 Kilogramm ausgesteinte Sauerkirschen

In 1 Liter kochende Milch rührt man so viel mittelfeinen Gries, daß man einen dicken Brei erhält, welcher unter fortgesetztem Umrühren glattgekocht wird und keine Klümpchen haben darf, worauf man ihn ausschüttet und erkalten läßt. Man reibt nun 250 Gramm Butter zu Schaum, thut allmählich zehn bis zwölf Eidotter, 125 Gramm gestoßene Mandeln, 160 Gramm Zucker, die abgeriebene Schale einer Zitrone, zwei Kaffeelöffel gestoßenen Zimmt, den Griesbrei, den Schnee von zehn Eiweißen und 1 Kilogramm ausgesteinte Sauerkirschen hinzu, füllt Alles in eine gebutterte Form und bäckt den Pudding eine reichliche Stunde bei mäßiger Hitze.

GÂTEAU DE SEMOULE AUX CERISES

1 litre de lait, semoule moyenne, 250 grammes de beurre, 10 à 12 œufs,
125 grammes de poudre d'amande, 160 grammes de sucre, zeste râpé d'un citron,
2 cuillères à café de cannelle en poudre, 1 kilogramme de griottes dénoyautées

Dans 1 litre de lait bouillant, versez en tournant sans arrêt suffisamment de semoule pour obtenir une bouillie assez ferme et lisse, sans grumeaux. Puis versez la préparation dans un plat et laissez refroidir. Battez ensuite 250 grammes de beurre jusqu'à ce qu'il soit mousseux, ajoutez peu à peu 10 à 12 jaunes d'œufs, 125 grammes d'amandes en poudre, 160 grammes de sucre, le zeste râpé d'un citron, 2 cuillerées à café de cannelle en poudre, la bouillie de semoule, les blancs d'œufs battus en neige et 1 kilogramme de griottes dénoyautées. Versez le tout dans un plat beurré et mettez à cuire le gâteau de semoule pendant une bonne heure à température moyenne.

PLATE X

George the Second's Cherry · Groffien or Biggarou · Harrison's Heart
Holländische Große Prinzessinkirsche · Groffien oder Biggarou · Harrison's Heart
Gros bigarreau de Princesse de Hollande · Bigarreau · Harrison's Heart

PLATE X.
Painted & Published as the Act directs by the Author G.Brookshaw May 1808.

PLATE XI

Tradescant Cherry · Millet's Duke · Amber Heart Cherry
Große Schwarze Knorpelkirsche · Frühe Herzogkirsche · Frühe Bernsteinkirsche
Bigarreau gros noir · Cerise précoce de mai · Guigne jaune

PLATE XII *(Page | Seite 64)*

Kentish or Flemish Cherry · English Bearer · Carnation Cherry
Flamentiner · Bleichrote Glaskirsche · Rote Oranienkirsche (Fleischfarbige Kirsche)
Flamentin · Cerise nouvelle d'Angleterre · Cerise rouge d'Orange

PLATE XIII *(Page | Seite 65)*

Morello · Caroon · Ronolds Black Heart
Brüsseler Braune · Englische Schwarze Kronenkirsche · Tartarische Schwarze Herzkirsche
Cerise guigne · Guigne de couronne · Cœur noir de Ronold

PLATE XI

Painted & Published as the Act directs by the Author G. Brookshaw June 1805.

PLATE XII.
Painted & Published as the Act directs by the Author G Brookshaw June 1st 1806

PLATE XIII.
Painted & Published as the Act directs by the Author, Brookshaw 1806.

PLUMS
Pflaumen | Prunes

Whatever tastes good is probably not healthy. That hard truth happily does not apply to plums. This delicious source of vitamins provides essential roughage for a weak digestion and was administered long before the doctor prescribed it to Molière's immortal hypochondriac, Monsieur Argan.

A member of the rose family, the plum tree profusely secretes gum-resin when injured. From its native home in western Asia it travelled via Greece to Italy, where it was cultivated and crossbred as early as the 2nd century B.C. Today it is proliferated practically worldwide from over 2000 breeding stations. The term plum is actually only a general designation for various species, some of them hardly distinguishable. The Round or Egg Plum is among them, of course. Its generally purplish blue fruits are divided by an obvious seam and are quite soft and very succulent when ripe. The stone is not easily separated from the flesh, however. The damson is named after the Syrian city of Damascus. The flesh of this elongated, oval fruit does not contain as much water as round plums and is hence firmer, a perfect fruit for tarts. The Reine Claude, or Queen Claudia, taking its name from the consort of the French king, Francis I, turns yellow-skinned with a blush of red, and the pulp loses its dark yellow colour to become yellowish-green, while retaining its full aroma and sweetness. Finally, the spherical little Mirabelles should also be mentioned as particularly well suited for stewing. Brignole Plums are not only good, long-lasting sweetmeats but, for the reasons mentioned above, are useful for their laxative qualities. The salutary benefits of plums cannot be used as an argument for another product, however: *šlivolica* or distilled plum liquor, since the high sugar content of the fruit mash is converted during fermentation and distillation into high concentrations of alcohol.

PLATE XIV

Cherry-Plum · Laurance Plum · French Orlean · Common Orlean
Myrobalane (Kirschpflaume) · Van Mons Königspflaume · Frühe Herrnpflaume · Common Orlean
— · Reine-Claude rouge de van Mons · Monsieur hâtive · —

PLATE XIV
Painted & Published as the Act directs by the Author G. Brookshaw June 1806

Was gut schmeckt, ist zumeist nicht gesund. Diese schmerzliche Erfahrung trifft erfreulicherweise auf die Pflaume keineswegs zu. Sie ist nicht nur ein leckerer Vitaminspender, ihre Ballaststoffe helfen auch der Verdauung nach und dies nicht erst seit ihrer ärztlichen Empfehlung an Monsieur Argan, dem von Molière unsterblich gemachten Eingebildeten Kranken.

Die Heimat der zu den Rosengewächsen zählenden Obstbäume, die bei Verletzungen ein auffälliges Gummiharz absondern, ist im westlichen Asien zu suchen. Von dort gelangten sie über Griechenland nach Italien, wo sie schon im 2. vorchristlichen Jahrhundert durch Kreuzung kultiviert wurden. Heute sind sie in über zweitausend Zuchtsorten praktisch weltweit verbreitet. Dabei ist der Begriff Pflaume eigentlich nur eine Sammelbezeichnung für verschiedene, teilweise schwer zu unterscheidende Arten. Natürlich gehört dazu zuerst die Echte Pflaume, auch Rund- oder Eierpflaume genannt. Ihre zumeist blau-violetten Früchte lassen eine deutliche Naht erkennen und sind zur Reifezeit relativ weich und sehr saftig. Der Stein löst sich allerdings nur schwer vom Fruchtfleisch. Als „Damaszener Pflaume", benannt nach dem syrischen Damaskus, wurde die dunkelblaue Zwetsch(g)e in Europa bekannt. Das Fruchtfleisch der länglicheren und spitz-oval zulaufenden Früchte enthält nicht so viel Wasser wie das der Rundpflaume, ist deshalb fester und als Kuchenbelag bestens geeignet. Bei den Renekloden, die ihren Namen nach Reine Claude, der Gattin des französischen Königs Franz I. erhielten, ändert sich die Farbe der Schale nach gelb mit einem mehr oder weniger deutlichen Anteil von Rot; und auch das Fruchtfleisch verliert seine dunkelgelbe Färbung und wird grünlich-gelb, bleibt aber überaus aromatisch und süß. Und schließlich wäre noch die kleine, ebenfalls gelbe und kugelige Mirabelle zu erwähnen, die sich besonders als Kochobst eignet. Trockenpflaumen sind nicht nur eine gut lagerfähige Form der Früchte, sie werden aus den oben bereits erwähnten Gründen zur Entschlackung verzehrt. Gesundheitlicher Nutzen lässt sich dagegen bei einer anderen Form verarbeiteter Zwetschgen nicht mehr als Argument anführen, denn das Zwetschgenwasser enthält den hohen Zuckeranteil der vermaischten Früchte nur noch in vergorener und durch Destillation konzentrierter Form als Alkohol.

PLATE XV

— · Morroco Plum · Precos de Tour · Purple Hâtive
— · Königspflaume aus Tours · Frühpflaume aus Tours · Frühe Rote Kaiserpflaume
— · Royale de Tours · Précoce de Tours · Impériale rouge hâtive

PLATE XV
Painted & Published as the Act directs by the Author G. Brookshaw May 1803.

Ce qui est bon au goût n'est souvent pas bon pour la santé. Fort heureusement, cette constatation douloureuse ne s'applique pas à la prune. Délicieuse, riche en vitamines, elle était déjà connue pour ses propriétés laxatives bien avant d'avoir été recommandée à Argan, le malade imaginaire immortalisé par Molière.

Entaillé, cet arbre fruitier de la famille des rosacées sécrète une gomme-résine très apparente. De l'Asie occidentale dont il est originaire, le prunier s'est répandu vers la Grèce et l'Italie où on le cultivait déjà par croisement au IIe siècle av. J.-C. Avec plus de 2000 variétés, cet arbre fruitier est pratiquement implanté aujourd'hui dans le monde entier. Cependant, le mot de prune n'est qu'un terme générique pour désigner de multiples variétés, parfois très difficiles à distinguer les unes des autres. Parmi celles-ci, on compte évidemment en premier lieu la prune proprement dite, de forme ronde ou ovoïde. Ce fruit, généralement d'un bleu violet, présente une très nette couture à sa surface, et à maturité, est relativement tendre et extrêmement juteux. Le noyau se détache difficilement de la chair. Connue d'abord sous le nom de « prune de Damas », la quetsche bleu foncé s'est à son tour répandue en Europe. La chair de ce fruit plus allongé, ovale ou pointu aux extrémités, ne contient pas autant d'eau que celle de la prune ronde. La plus grande fermeté de sa chair la prédestine aux fonds de tarte. Chez la reine-claude, nommée d'après l'épouse du roi François Ier, la couleur de la peau passe au jaune, avec une trace plus ou moins franche de rouge, et la chair perd sa coloration jaune foncé pour devenir jaune vert, mais le goût reste extrêmement parfumé et suave. Pour finir, il convient encore de mentionner la petite mirabelle, également jaune et toute ronde, qui se prête particulièrement à la cuisson. La prune se conserve bien sous sa forme séchée, ou pruneau, dont la consommation est recommandée pour un nettoyage du système digestif, comme nous l'avons déjà expliqué. Mais les motifs diététiques ne peuvent plus être invoqués pour justifier la consommation de l'eau-de-vie de prune, car la haute teneur en sucre du fruit pressé a été transformée en alcool par fermentation et distillation.

PLATE XVI.
Painted & Published as the Act directs by the Author G. Brookshaw July 1st, 1806.

72

PLATE XVII.
Painted & Published as the Act directs by the Author G. Brookshaw. June 1. 1806.

PLATE XVIII.
Painted & Published as the Act directs by the Author G. Brookshaw 1817.

PLATE XXI

Pear Plum · Blue Imperatrice · — · Brignole · St. Catharine
Weiße Birnpflaume · Blaue Kaiserin · — · Herrnpflaume · Gelbe Katharinenpflaume
Prune poire · Impératrice · — · Brignole (Monsieur Violet) · Prune de Sainte Catherine

PLATE XXII *(Page | Seite 76)*

Common Damson · — · White Damson · — · —
Damaszenerpflaume · Kleine Weiße Damaszenerpflaume · — · —
Damas · Petite Damas blanc · — · —

PLATE XXIII *(Page | Seite 77)*

Carnation Plum · Wine Sour Plum · Dauphine Plum
Carnation · — · Saure Weinpflaume von Yorkshire · Dauphinspflaume
— · — · Vincuse de Yorkshire · Reine-Claude ancienne (Prune Dauphine)

PLATE XXI.
London Published as the Act directs, by the Author, J. Brookshaw 1817

PLATE XXX.

PLATE XXIII.
Painted & Published as the Act directs by the Author G. Brookshaw August 1806.

APRICOTS
Aprikosen | Abricots

The botanical name *Prunus armeniaca* is geographically misleading since the true home of the apricot is not Armenia but much further to the east, in Manchuria and northern China. From there it moved westward to the Near East and thus into the vicinity of Persia and Armenia. They called it *praikokia* or *praecoquia* – "precocious" – because it ripens early in the year, and through the vagaries of language it later acquired its initial A to become known by its current name. The apricot first traversed the Alps with the Romans but the Moors in Spain also saw to its cultivation and from there the relatively small tree arrived in French gardens during the 15th century. Even so, the apricot remained a quite insignificant fruit until the 18th century. Not even its botanical classification was clear and, despite its distinct flavour, it was considered a variety of peach. The stones of some varieties are bitter-tasting and were – and sometimes still are – used as an almond substitute: in Austria the apricot is customarily known as *Marille*, from the Latin for bitter, *amarus*. In the 18th century the apricot tree also reached the Americas, where it is still being cultivated with success. The fruit is best eaten fresh, but is also popular canned or dried. Apricot jam is equally liked, and is a must in some baking recipes like the exquisite Viennese chocolate *Sachertorte;* and the *Marillen-Schnaps* from Austria and Hungary makes a nice digestive after a helping of *Marillen* dumplings, a delicious traditional Austrian dessert.

Ihr botanischer Name, *Prunus armeniaca*, führt geographisch auf einen Umweg, denn die eigentliche Heimat der Aprikose liegt nicht in Armenien, sondern sehr viel weiter östlich, in der Mandschurei und im Norden Chinas. Von dort kam sie nach Westen bis in den Vorderen Orient und damit auch in das persisch-armenische Gebiet. Wegen ihrer frühen Reifezeit wurde sie „praikokia" und „praecoquia", genannt, was später auf verschlungenen Wegen und mit vorgesetztem A zum heute gebräuchlichen deutschen Namen führte. Daneben ist insbesondere in Österreich auch die Bezeichnung „Marille" gebräuchlich. Durch die Römer kam die Aprikose erstmals über die Alpen, aber auch die Mauren sorgten später in Spanien für ihren Anbau und von dort gelangte der relativ kleine Baum im 15. Jahrhundert auch in französische Gärten. Trotzdem blieb die Aprikose als Obst bis ins 18. Jahrhundert ziemlich bedeutungslos, zumal man sich über ihre botanische Einordnung zuerst nicht im Klaren war und sie trotz des unterschiedlichen Geschmacks für eine Pfirsichart hielt. Die bei manchen Sorten bitter schmeckenden Steine wurden und werden vereinzelt als Mandelersatz verwendet. Im 18. Jahrhundert gelangte der Aprikosenbaum auch nach Amerika, wo er noch immer mit gutem Ertrag kultiviert wird. Die Früchte werden gerne frisch gegessen, sind aber auch als Saftkonserve und als Trockenobst beliebt. Das gilt auch für die Marmelade, die z.B. in der Sachertorte nicht fehlen darf, und insbesondere in Österreich und Ungarn für den Marillen-Schnaps, der sich z.B. nach einem typisch österreichischen Dessert empfiehlt: leckeren Marillenknödeln.

Son nom botanique, *prunus armeniaca*, nous induit en erreur sur sa véritable origine géographique, qui n'est pas l'Arménie mais se situe beaucoup plus à l'est, en Mandchourie et au nord de la Chine. De là, l'abricot a progressé vers l'Occident jusqu'au Proche-Orient, en passant par la Perse et l'Arménie. A cause de sa maturité précoce, il fut appelé « praikokia », et « praecoquia », ce qui a conduit, par déformations successives et positionnement de la lettre « A » en début de mot, au nom français actuel. En Autriche, on trouve aussi la désignation de « marille ». Avec les Romains, l'abricot a franchi les Alpes. Les Maures l'ont implanté par la suite en Espagne, d'où cet arbre, relativement petit, a gagné les jardins français du XVe siècle. Jusqu'au XVIIIe siècle, l'abricot n'a pas suscité un grand intérêt alimentaire, dans la mesure où l'on ne savait pas dans quelle catégorie botanique le classer et qu'on le tenait plutôt pour une variété de pêche, malgré son goût fort différent. Les noyaux qui, chez certaines variétés, ont un goût amer, étaient et sont encore parfois utilisés à la place de l'amande. Au XVIIIe siècle, l'abricotier a aussi été implanté en Amérique où il est toujours cultivé avec un bon rendement. L'abricot est volontiers consommé frais, mais aussi apprécié en conserve et en fruit sec. Il est également transformé en confiture, ingrédient essentiel du célèbre « Sachertorte », gâteau viennois au chocolat et à la confiture d'abricot, et en « Marillen-Schnaps », eau-de-vie aux abricots qui se déguste très volontiers, notamment en Hongrie et en Autriche, après un dessert typiquement autrichien tel que les délicieuses boulettes aux abricots, dites « Marillenknödel ».

PLATE XIX

White Masculine · Red Masculine · Orange Apricot · Turkish Apricot
Kleine Weiße Frühaprikose · Frühe Muskateller-Aprikose · Orangen-Aprikose · Türkische Aprikose
Abricot blanc · Abricot hâtif musqué · Orange précoce · Gros abricot

PLATE XIX

Painted & Published as the Act directs by the Author G Brookshaw June 1804.

APRICOT CHARLOTTE

12–15 fine apricots, not over ripe, 3 oz sugar, a lump of fresh butter,
slices of French bread or rusk

Peel and halve twelve to fifteen fine apricots, not over ripe, and allow them to simmer in three ounces of sugar and a lump of fresh butter for a quarter of an hour, stirring frequently; next brush the baking pan with melted butter, dip the slices of French bread or rusk first in melted butter, then in sugar; use them to line the bottom and sides of the pan closely; tip the apricots inside and cover them with more such slices of French bread, dust with sugar and bake in a hot oven from a half to three quarters of an hour.

APRIKOSEN-CHARLOTTE

12–15 schöne, nicht zu reife Aprikosen, 80 Gramm Zucker,
ein kleines Stück frischer Butter, Scheiben von Milchbrod oder Einback

Zwölf bis fünfzehn schöne, nicht zu reife Aprikosen werden geschält, halbirt und mit 80 Gramm Zucker nebst einem kleinen Stück frischer Butter eine Viertelstunde lang unter öfterem Umschütteln gedämpft. Dann streicht man die Form mit geschmolzener Butter aus, taucht Scheiben von Milchbrod oder Einback erst in geschmolzene Butter, dann in Zucker, legt die Form auf dem Boden und an den Seiten dicht damit aus, schüttet die Aprikosen hinein, bedeckt dieselben mit ebensolchen Milchbrodscheiben, bestreut sie mit Zucker und bäckt sie in einem heißen Ofen eine halbe bis drei Viertelstunden lang.

CHARLOTTE AUX ABRICOTS

12–15 beaux abricots pas trop mûrs, 80 grammes de sucre,
un petit morceau de beurre frais, quelques tranches de pain au lait ou autre gâteau au lait

Pelez douze à quinze beaux abricots pas trop mûrs, coupez-les en deux et faites-les cuire à l'étuvée dans 80 grammes de sucre et un petit morceau de beurre frais pendant un quart d'heure en remuant de temps en temps. Beurrez le moule avec du beurre fondu. Puis trempez les tranches de pain au lait ou de gâteau au lait d'abord dans du beurre fondu puis dans du sucre, et disposez-les, serrées, dans le fond du moule et contre le bord. Sur ce lit de tranches, déposez les abricots, recouvrez-les de nouvelles tranches de pain au lait préparées de la dite manière, saupoudrez de sucre et faites cuire le tout dans un four chaud pendant une demi-heure, trois quarts d'heure.

PLATE XX

Black Apricot · Breda Apricot · Brussels Moor Park Apricot · —
Die Schwarze Aprikose · Aprikose aus Breda (Holländische Aprikose) · Pfirsichaprikose · —
Abricot noir · Abricot de Hollande (Abricot de Breda) · Moorpark · —

PLATE XX.

London Published as the Act directs by the Author, J. Brookshaw, December 1, 1817.

PEACHES · NECTARINES
Pfirsiche · Nektarinen | Pêches · Nectarines

Although its botanical name *prunus persica* points to Persia, in reality the peach originates from China and picked up the name on a stopover along its way west, whence the Romans came to know and appreciate it. Pliny, of course, also records it, and from him we learn that the plant was supposed to originate with Perseus, son of Danaë and Zeus, who appeared to her in the form of a shower of gold. He also tells us that a descendant of that demigod, Alexander the Great, personally crowned the victors at the games in Memphis with wreathes of peach branches.

In Egypt, however, these sensitive trees did not grow very well, because the plant needs a definite chill during its winter dormancy as part of its growing cycle. It prefers temperate climes, which explains why the French peach has gained such a high reputation. It was Roman troops who first brought these downy delights to Germany, where cultivation has continued in places on a small scale to this day.

In the 17th century peaches crossed the Atlantic and encountered very good growing conditions on American soil. Consequently, in our times, the USA has become the main producer on the world market, with the yellow-fleshed fruits the dominant variety. The white-fleshed varieties are a little more flavorful, but generally ripen later. They include the Bloody Peach, despite its striking name and dark-red, juicy pulp. A cross between peach and plum led to a hybrid of lasting importance, the very popular nectarine. Besides its somewhat firmer consistency owing to a lower water content, it differs from the dessert or fuzzy peach primarily by its smooth skin. Both nectarines and peaches have clingstone varieties, so called because the stone is difficult to separate from the flesh. Once ripe, no varieties keep long and they are particularly susceptible to bruising. So they provide gourmets with a welcome excuse for immediate consumption. And now at last we should think of the Australian coloratura soprano Helen Litchell (1861–1931). In 1900 the brilliant chef Auguste Escoffier devised a dessert in her honour, a combination of peaches, raspberries, and vanilla ice-cream. She adopted the stage-name of Nellie Melba, and named after her thus, the dessert became world-famous as Peach Melba.

PLATE XXIV

Red Nutmeg · Hemskirk Peach · — · —
Kleiner Roter Frühpfirsich · Pfirisch von Hemskirk · — · —
Avant pêche rouge · — · —

PLATE XXIV.
Painted & Published as the Act directs by the Author G. Brookshaw, April 1806.

Sein botanischer Name *prunus persica* deutet zwar auf Persien hin, in Wirklichkeit stammt der Pfirsich jedoch aus China und behielt lediglich auf seiner Wanderung Richtung Westen den Namen dieser Durchgangsstation bei, auf der ihn auch die Römer kennen und schätzen lernten. Natürlich berichtet Plinius über ihn und so erfahren wir, dass die Pflanze auf Perseus, den Sohn des goldregnenden Zeus und der Danae, zurückgehen soll, und dass ein später Nachkomme des Halbgottes, Alexander der Große, eigenhändig die Sieger der Spiele von Memphis mit Kränzen aus Pfirsichzweigen krönte.

In Ägypten wuchsen die recht anfälligen Bäume allerdings nicht allzu gut, denn die Pflanze braucht in ihrem Vegetationszyklus eine deutliche Winterpause. Gemäßigte Klimate bekommen ihr besser, was den Ruf der hochgelobten französischen Pfirsiche erklärt. Nach Deutschland, wo sich ihr Anbau stellenweise bis heute im kleinen Stil erhalten hat, gelangten die pelzigen Köstlichkeiten durch die römischen Truppen.

Im 17. Jahrhundert übersprang der Pfirsich den Atlantik. Da ihm Amerika sehr gute Wuchsbedingungen bot, wurden die USA in unserer Zeit zu einem der wichtigsten Produzenten des Welthandels, auf dem die gelbfleischigen Früchte dominieren. Noch etwas geschmacksintensiver sind die weißfleischigen Sorten, die allerdings zumeist später reifen. Zu ihnen zählt, dem Namen zum Trotz, auch der Blutpfirsich, der nicht nur mehr Saft führt, sondern in erster Linie durch sein dunkelrot gefärbtes Fruchtfleisch verblüfft. Von nachhaltiger Bedeutung erwies sich die Kreuzung des Pfirsichs mit der Pflaume, die zur heute sehr beliebten Nektarine führte. Neben einem etwas festeren, weil wasserärmeren Fruchtfleisch unterscheidet sie sich vom Edel- oder Pelz-Pfirsich vor allem durch ihre glatte Fruchthaut. Diese hat sie auch mit den aromatischen Brugnolen gemeinsam, deren Stein sich allerdings nur schwer vom Fruchtfleisch löst, eine Eigenschaft, die diese mit den Pfirsich-Härtlingen, auch Duranzen genannt, teilen. Im reifen Zustand sind alle Sorten nur sehr beschränkt haltbar und vor allem sehr druckempfindlich. Feinschmeckern bieten sie dadurch die gern genutzte Möglichkeit, für alsbaldigen Verzehr zu sorgen. Und spätestens jetzt sollten wir an Helen Litchell (1861–1931) denken, deren Name sich untrennbar mit dem Pfirsich verbindet. Zu ihren Ehren komponierte der geniale Koch Auguste Escoffier im Jahr 1900 ein Dessert aus Pfirsich, Himbeeren und Vanilleeis, das mit dem Künstlernamen der australischen Koloratursopranistin – Nellie Melba – weltberühmt wurde: Pfirsich Melba.

PLATE XXV

White Avant Peach · Bears Red Avant · White Magdalen · Red Magdalen
Kleiner Weißer Frühpfirsich · Früher Purpurpfirsich · Weißer Magdalenen-Pfirsich · Roter Magdalenen-Pfirsich
Avant blanche · Avant rouge · Madeleine blanche (Montagne blanche) · Madeleine rouge (Madeleine de Courson)

PLATE XXV.
Painted & Published as the Act directs by the Author G. Brookshaw. June 1st 1806.

Sa dénomination botanique *prunus persica* renvoie à la Perse, mais en réalité, la pêche est originaire de Chine et n'a gardé dans son nom que le souvenir d'une étape de son voyage vers l'Occident. C'est toutefois en Perse que les Romains ont appris à la connaître et à l'apprécier. Pline en parle évidemment, et en fait remonter l'origine à Persée, fils de Danaé et de Zeus métamorphosé en pluie d'or. Alexandre le Grand, descendant lointain du demi-dieu Persée, aurait, de sa propre main, décoré d'une couronne de branches de pêcher les vainqueurs des jeux de Memphis.

En Egypte, cependant, le pêcher fragile poussait moins bien car il a besoin de marquer, dans son cycle végétatif, une véritable pause hivernale. Les climats tempérés lui conviennent mieux, ce qui explique la renommée des pêches françaises. Les Allemands doivent aux troupes romaines l'introduction dans leur pays de ce fruit délicieux à la peau veloutée, mais sa culture y reste rare. Au XVIIe siècle, la pêche traverse l'Atlantique et trouve d'excellentes conditions de croissance en Amérique.

Aujourd'hui, les Etats-Unis sont devenus l'un des plus importants producteurs de pêche au monde, les variétés à chair jaune étant les plus représentées. Celles à chair blanche ont un goût plus intense mais mûrissent généralement plus tard. Curieusement, on compte parmi elles la pêche sanguine, plus juteuse, qui fascine par sa chair d'un rouge profond. Le croisement de la pêche avec la prune a donné la nectarine, très appréciée aujourd'hui. Elle se distingue de la pêche à la peau veloutée par une chair un peu plus ferme, car moins gorgée d'eau, et surtout par sa peau lisse. C'est une caractéristique qu'elle partage avec le brugnon, très parfumé, mais dont le noyau se détache difficilement de la chair, comme c'est aussi la cas de la pêche dure, ou durance. Une fois mûres, toutes ces sortes souffrent d'une durée de conservation limitée et surtout, sont très sensibles aux chocs. C'est pourquoi elles demandent à être consommées sans tarder, invitation à laquelle les gourmets répondent bien volontiers. C'est ici le moment d'évoquer le nom de Helen Litchell (1861–1931), indissociablement lié à celui de la pêche. En son honneur, un cuisinier génial, Auguste Escoffier, inventa en 1900 un dessert composé de pêche, de framboise et de glace à la vanille qu'il baptisa «pêche Melba», du nom d'artiste de cette soprano colorature australienne – Nellie Melba –, et que ce dessert a rendu aujourd'hui mondialement connu.

PLATE XXVI

Grimwood's Royal George Peach · Grimwood's Royal Charlotte Peach · French Mignonne
Grimwoods Königliche Magdalene · Mittelgroßblühende Magdalene · Gemeiner Lieblingspfirsich (Lackpfirsich)
Madeleine rouge · Madeleine hâtive · Mignonne ordinaire

PLATE XXVI.
Painted & Published as the Act directs by the Author G.Brookshaw. April. 1805.

PLATE XXVII

Early Purple Peach · Peach of Mr. Padley's · Galand Peach (Violet Hâtive Peach)
Früher Purpurpfirsich · Peach of Mr. Padley's · Violette Galande
Pourprée hâtive · Peach of Mr. Padley's · Violette hâtive

PLATE XXVII.
Painted & Published at the Art Library by the Author G. Brookshaw. July 1st 1806.

PLATE XXVIII

Early Newington Peach · Buckinghamshire Mignonne · Mignonne Barrington Peach
Früher Newington (Frühe Dunkelrote Nektarine) · Mignon-Pfirsich von Buckinghamshire · Barringtoner Lieblingspfirsich
Nectarine de Newington · Mignonne de Buckinghamshire · Pêche de Barrington

PLATE XXIX *(Page | Seite 92)*

Montauban Peach · Gross Minion · Royal George Old Peach
Bergpfirsich · Großer Lieblingspfirsich (Lackpfirsich, Großer Prinzessinpfirsich) · Königspfirsich Old George
La Montauban · Grosse mignonne (Veloutée de Merlet) · Royal George Old Peach

PLATE XXVIII
Painted & Published as the Act directs by the Author G. Brookshaw. September 1st 1806.

PLATE XXX.
Painted & Published As the Act directs by the Author G. Brookshaw June 1806.

PLATE XXXI.
Painted & Published as the Act directs by the Author G. Brookshaw. June 1806

PEACH FRITTERS, AMERICAN

Peach halves marinated in sugar, batter: a cup of flour, 2 eggs,
2 teaspoonful of olive oil, 2 tablespoonful of brandy, some sugar

Prepare the batter the day before from a heaped cup of flour, the yolks of two eggs, two teaspoonful of olive oil and two tablespoonful of brandy or wine; on the day of use stir the batter well and gradually add enough cold water till it is viscous. Fold in the stiffly beaten whites of two eggs and dip the peach halves, which have been marinated for two hours in some wine or brandy and a generous amount of sugar and properly dripped dry, into the mixture and fry on both sides in hot butter or sizzling lard. Drain well on blotting paper, dust with sugar and send to table.

PFIRSICH-FRITTERS, AMERIKANISCH

In Zucker marinierte Pfirsichhälften, Backteig: Obertasse Mehl,
2 Eier, 2 Teelöffel Olivenöl, 2 Eßlöffel Brandy, etwas Zucker

Nachdem man Tags zuvor den Backteig aus einer gehäuften Obertasse Mehl, 2 Eidottern, 2 Löffeln Olivenöl, 2 Eßlöffeln Brandy oder Wein bereitet und durch gutes Umrühren sowie allmähliches Zugießen, von ein wenig kaltem Wasser zu einem dickflüssigem Teig gemacht hat, vermischt man ihn am Tage des Gebrauchs mit dem steifen Schnee der beiden Eiweiße, taucht die zwei Stunden in etwas Wein oder Brandy mit reichlichem Zucker marinierten und gehörig abgetropften Pfirsichhälften hinein, bäckt sie in heißer Butter oder kochendem Speck auf beiden Seiten, läßt sie gut auf Fließpapier ablaufen, bestreut sie mit Zucker und serviert sie.

BEIGNETS AUX PÊCHES AMÉRICAINS

Moitiés de pêches marinées dans du sucre, pâte : 1 tasse de farine,
2 œufs, 2 cuillerées à café d'huile d'olive, 2 cuillerées à soupe de brandy, un peu de sucre

Préparez la pâte la veille en mélangeant une tasse de farine, 2 jaunes d'œufs, 2 cuillerées d'huile d'olive et 2 cuillerées à soupe de brandy ou de vin. Mélangez bien en ajoutant progressivement un peu d'eau froide, jusqu'à obtenir une pâte épaisse. Le lendemain incorporez les blancs d'œufs battus en neige et trempez les moitiés de pêches soigneusement égouttées dans la préparation. Elles doivent avoir macéré pendant deux heures dans un peu de vin ou de brandy, additionné d'une quantité suffisante de sucre. Faites frire des deux côtés dans du beurre chaud ou de la graisse bouillante, laissez bien égoutter sur du papier buvard, saupoudrez de sucre et servez aussitôt.

PLATE XXXII

Marlborough Peach · Rombullion Peach · Double Mountain Peach
Marlborough-Pfirsich · Rombullion-Pfirsich · Doppelte Montagne (Großer Bergpfirsich)
Pêche de Marlborough · Rombullion · Double montagne (Montagne précoce la grosse)

PLATE XXXII.
Painted & Published as the Act directs by the Author G. Brookshaw 1807.

PLATE XXXIII

Black Peach of Montreal · Cambra Peach · Monshien's Pacey of Pomperi (Pavie of Pompone?)
Black Peach of Montreal · Cambra Peach · Monströser Lieblingspfirsich?
— · — · Pavie monstrueux?

PLATE XXXIV (*Page | Seite 100*)

Vermash Nectarine · Violet Hâtive Nectarine · Roman Nectarine · North's Scarlet Nectarine · Elrouge Nectarine · Peterborough Nectarine
Kleine Frühe Violette · Große Frühe Violette · Blutrote Nektarine (Römische Nektarine) · North's Scarlet Nectarine · Elrouge Nektarine (Englische Violette) · Peterborough Nectarine
Petite violette hâtive · Grosse violette hâtive · Brugnon violet musqué · — · Nectarine Elrouge · —

PLATE XXXV (*Page | Seite 101*)

Bourdine Peach · Nevet Peach · Late Admirable Peach
Burdins Lackpfirsich · Wollige Nivette (Sammetpfirsich) · Schöne aus Vitry
Bourdine royale · Pêche Nivette · Admirable tardive (Belle de Vitry)

PLATE XXXIV
Painted & Published as the Act directs by the Author G Brookshaw 1801

PLATE XXXV.
Painted & Published as the Act directs by the Author G. Brookshaw. Feby. 1812.

PLATE XXXVI

Chancellor Peach · Catherine Peach · Old Newington Peach
Kanzlerpfirsich · Katharinen-Lackpfirsich · Newingtons Magdalene (Härtling von Newington)
Chancelière · Belle Catherine · Pavie de Newington

PLATE XXXVII *(Page | Seite 104)*

Dutillees Nectarine · Brugnon's Old Nectarine · Brugnon's Round Nectarine · Murray Nectarine · Newington Nectarine
Dutillees Nectarine · Brugnon's Old Nectarine · Brugnon's Round Nectarine · Murray Nektarine · Newingtons Glattpfirsich
— · — · — · — · Brugnon de Newington

PLATE XXXVIII *(Page | Seite 105)*

— · Homerton's White Nectarine · Ford's Black Nectarine · Italian Nectarine
— · Homertons Weiße Nektarine · Fords Schwarze Nektarine · Italienische Nektarine
— · — · Brugnon noir de Ford · Brugnon d'Italie

PLATE XXXVI.
Painted & Published as the Act directs by the Author G. Brookshaw September 1817

PLATE XXVIII.
Engraved & Published as the Act directs by the Author G. Brookshaw 1817.

PINEAPPLES

Ananas | Ananas

Christopher Columbus and his sailors were the first Europeans to become acquainted with pineapples. When they landed on Guadeloupe in 1493, they received these spiny fruits originally native to Brazil as a gift from their hosts. Brought to the court of King Ferdinand and Queen Isabella in Spain, they delighted Their Majesties not only with their unusual appearance, but particularly with their unique flavour. For a long time pineapples remained the privilege of a few, appearing in the gardens and on the tables only of those of high rank or great wealth. Sailors occasionally had the chance to eat the exotic fruit on board ship, however, as an antidote to the dreaded scurvy.

It was relatively simple to cultivate, since a new plant could be raised with little effort from the severed crown, which could be brought to fruitbearing maturity even in the hothouses of central Europe. The Spaniards and Portuguese soon began to plant pineapples in their colonies; thus they arrived in Africa and Asia as early as around 1550. But transportation from there to Europe still posed major problems since many of the fruits rotted during the long journeys. It was only with the introduction of steamships with their more predictable travel times that the overseas trade could gradually develop. Candying was one way to extend the storage life of the fruit. Especially in the 18th century, the whole pineapple was preferentially conserved in sugar to preserve its characteristic shape. Its resemblance to a large pinecone consequently led to its English name, while the French or German term *ananas* derives from its original designations *nana* and *anana* in the South American Guaraní language.

The breakthrough for pineapples as a product on the global market came at the end of the 19th century when they were conserved, ready to eat, in cans. Canning was instituted in Singapore in 1888, in Hawaii in 1892, and in Formosa in 1902. The Ginaca machine, developed in 1913 in Hawaii, soon enabled fully automated peeling and coring of the pineapple, and the fleshy cylinder could then be sliced or cut into chunks as desired. Today this tropical fruit is dispersed worldwide and is available at a reasonable price. Nevertheless, the opinion that Michael Friedrich Lochner expressed in 1714 still applies: the pineapple "should be called a queen of the fruits, which embraces all the delights of the palate."

PLATE XL

Black Jamaica Pine

—

—

PLATE XL.

Black Jamaica

Drawn & Pub. by the Author G. Brookshaw.

Christoph Columbus und seine Matrosen waren die ersten Europäer, die die Ananas kennen lernten. Als sie 1493 auf Guadeloupe landeten, erhielten sie die ursprünglich in Brasilien beheimateten stacheligen Früchte als Gastgeschenk. Nach Spanien an den Hof König Ferdinands gebracht, erregten sie nicht nur durch ihr ungewöhnliches Aussehen, sondern insbesondere durch ihren unvergleichlichen Geschmack das Wohlgefallen der Majestäten. Den Gärten und Tafeln hoch gestellter und wohlhabender Personen blieb die Ananas lange Zeit vorbehalten, nur manche Matrosen hatten Glück, wenn auf ihren Schiffen der Genuss der exotischen Frucht den gefürchteten Skorbut verhindern sollte.

Der Anbau war relativ einfach möglich, denn aus der abgetrennten Krone ließ sich mit geringem Aufwand eine neue Pflanze ziehen, die auch in Mitteleuropa in Treibhäusern zur Fruchtreife gebracht werden konnte. Von den Spaniern und den Portugiesen wurde die Ananas schon bald in den Kolonien angepflanzt und kam so bereits um 1550 nach Afrika und Asien. Allerdings bereitete der Transport von dort nach Europa noch große Probleme, da viele Früchte auf den langen Reisen verdarben. Erst mit Einführung der Dampfschiffe, deren Fahrtdauer berechenbarer war, konnte sich der Überseehandel nach und nach entfalten. Eine längere Verwendbarkeit der Früchte ließ sich auch durch Kandieren erreichen, wobei besonders im 18. Jahrhundert gerne die ganzen Früchte mit Zucker konserviert wurden. So blieb das charakteristische Aussehen erhalten, das an einen großen Kiefern- oder Pinienzapfen erinnert und folgerichtig im Englischen zur Bezeichnung „pineapple" führte, während sich „Ananas" vom ursprünglichen „nana" und „anana" in der südamerikanischen Guarani-Sprache ableitet.

Der Durchbruch der Ananas als Weltwirtschaftsgut begann am Ende des 19. Jahrhunderts, als man sie 1888 in Singapur, 1892 auf Hawaii und 1902 auf Formosa essfertig in Dosen konservierte. Die 1913 auf Hawaii entwickelte Ginaca-Maschine erlaubte bald die vollautomatische Schälung und Entkernung der Ananas, deren zylindrisch zugeschnittenes Fruchtfleisch nach Wunsch in Scheiben oder Stücke zerteilt werden konnte. Heute ist die tropische Frucht weltweit verbreitet und zum preiswerten Obst geworden, aber immer noch gilt Michael Friedrich Lochners 1714 geäußerte Meinung, die Ananas sei „eine Königin der Früchte zu nennen, in welche alle Lustreizungen des Geschmacks versenket".

PLATE XLI

Riply Pine

—

Plate 41.

Repby Pine

Painted and Published as the Act directs, by the Author, G. Brookshaw.

Christophe Colomb et ses matelots furent les premiers Européens à découvrir l'ananas. Lorsqu'ils débarquèrent en Guadeloupe en 1493, ce fruit écailleux, originaire du Brésil, leur fut offert en cadeau d'accueil. A la Cour du roi Ferdinand d'Espagne, l'aspect insolite de l'ananas, et surtout sa saveur incomparable, surent plaire à Leurs Majestés. Longtemps réservé aux jardins et aux tables des personnes de haut rang et de grande fortune, ce fruit exotique protégeait parfois du scorbut tant redouté un équipage qui avait la chance d'en consommer. La culture en était relativement facile.

Il suffisait de couper la touffe de feuilles à son sommet pour faire naître une nouvelle plante qui mûrissait même dans les serres d'Europe centrale. Les Espagnols et les Portugais ne mirent pas longtemps à l'implanter dans leurs colonies et dès 1550, on le voit mûrir en Afrique et en Asie. Cependant, le transport jusqu'en Europe posait problème. Beaucoup de fruits se gâtaient pendant la traversée. Quand la durée des voyages devint plus prévisible avec l'introduction des bateaux à vapeur, ce négoce maritime put se développer progressivement. Glacés, ou entièrement confits dans du sucre, comme cela se pratiquait surtout au XVIIIᵉ siècle, l'ananas se conservait plus longtemps et gardait sa forme caractéristique de pomme de pin. C'est à elle qu'il doit d'ailleurs son nom anglais de « pineapple » alors que dans d'autres langues, la dénomination « ananas » est dérivée du mot primitif « nana » ou « anana » donné par les indiens Guaranis d'Amérique du Sud.

L'ananas s'imposa véritablement sur le marché mondial à la fin du XIXᵉ siècle, à partir du moment où l'on sut le conserver en boîte, prêt à être consommé : en 1888 à Singapour, en 1892 à Hawaii et en 1902 à Formose. Bientôt, la machine Ginaca, développée à Hawaii en 1913, en automatisa complètement l'épluchage et l'évidage. Sa chair, taillée dans une forme cylindrique par la machine, pouvait ensuite être découpée en rondelles ou en morceaux, selon les besoins. Aujourd'hui, ce fruit tropical est répandu dans le monde entier à un prix abordable. Mais l'opinion émise en 1714 à son sujet par Michael Friedrich Lochner reste encore valable. Il faut, disait-il, « l'appeler roi des fruits, tant se fondent en lui toutes les jouissances du palais ».

PLATE XLIII

Brown Havannah Pine

—

—

PLATE XLIV (*Page | Seite 112*)

Smoothe Leaved Green Antigua Pine

—

—

PLATE XLV (*Page | Seite 113*)

Jagged Leaf Black Antigua

—

—

PLATE XLIII.
Painted & Published by the Author G. Brookshaw 1807.

Brown Havannah.

PLATE XLIV.

Printed & Published as the Act directs by the Author C.Brookshaw 1817

PLATE LV.

Black Antigua.

Painted & Pub. by the Author G. Brookshaw.

GRAPES
Trauben | Raisins

Grapes can, of course, be eaten fresh – but why? This blasphemous statement, or something similar, might well come out of the mouth of a wine enthusiast. You can see what he means, but at the same time you can see what pleasures of the palate that disciple of Bacchus is glibly depriving himself of. There are good reasons why the breeding of grapes pursues different goals, depending on whether they are destined for the wine-press or the dessert-bowl. What matters for wine grapes is the taste and bouquet that the fruits give to the finished wine. Dessert grapes, on the other hand, must pay equal tribute to the eye and the palate: attractive, plump clusters, preferably seedless and tender-skinned and, of course, full of flavour.

Back to the beverage grapes: for at least 6000 years mankind has known how to prepare grape juice so as to allow yeast to ferment the sugar into alcohol. The wine produced then probably tasted quite different from what we are used to today, but it was evidently quite popular in Asia Minor and in Egypt, for example, and also created much demand among the Greeks. Their characteristic resin-flavoured wine, *retsina*, is still liked to this day. The Romans spread viticulture throughout Europe. Even the Church played an important role during medieval times, since Jesus' words, "I am the vine, ye are the branches" (John 15.5) elevated the plant to a symbolic importance that explains its intense cultivation in monasteries. But it was only in the 18th century that viticulture as we now know it was gradually developed. There was a severe setback around the middle of the 19th century, however, when the vine pest *phylloxera*, a species of louse, was imported from America. It ravaged the European stocks, causing much worse damage than the more familiar mildews. American varieties were more resistant to the destructive pest, but the flavour of their wines could not quite satisfy discerning German winegrowers and wine lovers. Finally, a way was found to outsmart the louse: since it only attacked the roots of the European vines, well-tried varieties were simply grafted onto immune American rootstocks. As a consequence of this preventive measure, grape varieties have proliferated profusely ever since. But with some effort anyone will eventually find the grape to suit his or her taste, without being limited to the classical viticultures of Italy, Spain, France or Germany. For the selection today hails from all parts of the world, from South Africa to the Americas. There are countless white, rosé and red wines, whose colour is determined by the fermentation process: white wines are made from the must of green or yellow grapes, rosés are produced from the juice of red grapes, and red wines are made from the mash of red or blue varieties, fermented together with the skins to define the colour. The final product with its healthy natural ingredients, when taken in sensible moderation, makes for a very tasty cordial.

PLATE XLVII

Reasin de Calmes
Reasin de Calmes
Raisin de Calmes

PLATE XLVII

Raisin de Calmes

Natürlich kann man Trauben auch frisch essen, aber warum sollte man? Ein ketzerischer Satz, den man so oder so ähnlich aus dem Mund eines überzeugten Weintrinkers hören könnte. Man erkennt, was er damit meint, man erkennt aber zugleich auch, dass sich der Bacchusjünger selbst leichtfertig um eine Gaumenfreude bringt. Nicht umsonst verfolgt die Züchtung der zum Keltern bestimmten Reben und der Tafeltrauben verschiedene Ziele. Bei den Wein-Trauben kommt es allein auf den Geschmack an, den die Früchte dem fertigen Wein verleihen. Bei den Tafeltrauben aber fordern Auge und Zunge gemeinsam ihren Tribut: imponierendes Aussehen, möglichst Kernlosigkeit, eine zarte Schale und natürlich das Aroma sind hier gleichermaßen gefragt.

Zurück zu den getrunkenen Trauben: Seit mindestens 6000 Jahren ist der Mensch in der Lage, mit dem Traubensaft so zu verfahren, dass dessen Zucker der Hefe Gelegenheit zur alkoholischen Gärung gibt. Der damals entstandene Wein schmeckte zwar sicherlich ganz anders, als wir dies heute gewöhnt sind, er fand aber zum Beispiel im Vorderen Orient und in Ägypten offenbar viele Anhänger und auch die Griechen sprachen ihm gerne zu. Ihr charakteristisch geharzter Wein, der Retsina, ist bis heute beliebt. Mit den Römern verbreitete sich der Rebanbau in Europa. Im Mittelalter spielte nicht zuletzt auch die Kirche eine wichtige Rolle, denn das Jesuswort „ich bin der Weinstock, ihr seid die Reben" (Joh. 15,5) erhebt die Pflanze zu besonderer symbolischer Bedeutung und macht ihre starke Kultur in den Klöstern verständlich. Erst im 18. Jahrhundert beginnt aber nach und nach der Ausbau der Weine auf die uns heute bekannte Weise. Um die Mitte des 19. Jahrhunderts kam es allerdings zu einem herben Rückschlag, als aus Amerika die Reblaus eingeschleppt wurde, die noch stärker als der altbekannte Mehltau die europäischen Bestände gefährdete. Die amerikanischen Sorten waren zwar gegen den lästigen Eindringling immun, aber der Geschmack ihres Weins konnte die deutschen Winzer und Weinliebhaber nicht so recht befriedigen. Abhilfe konnte dann aber ein Trick schaffen: Da die Reblaus nur die Wurzeln der europäischen Rebstöcke angriff, pfropfte man die bewährten Sorten einfach auf immune amerikanische Stöcke als Unterlage. Die Zahl der Rebsorten ist nicht zuletzt dank dieser Abwehrmaßnahme mittlerweile unüberschaubar geworden. Aber jeder, der sich darum bemüht, wird „seinen" Tropfen finden und er kann sich dazu nicht nur in den klassischen Anbauländern Italien, Spanien, Frankreich oder Deutschland umsehen, sondern hat heute von Südafrika bis Amerika und noch in manch anderen Regionen dieser Erde die Auswahl zwischen zahllosen weißen, rosé und roten Weinen, deren Farbe das Gärverfahren bestimmt: Weißweine entstehen aus dem gepressten Most grüner oder gelber Trauben, Roséweine aus dem Saft roter Trauben und Rotweine aus der Maische roter bzw. blauer Trauben, die zusammen mit den die Farbe bestimmenden Schalen vergoren wird. Wegen der darin enthaltenen Naturstoffe kann insbesondere Rotwein, mit Verstand und in Maßen genossen, sogar wohl schmeckende Arznei sein.

PLATE XLVIII

Royal Muscadine Grape
Weißer Gutedel (Gemeiner Gutedel)
Chasselas

PLATE XLVIII.

Royal Muscadine

Painted & Pub. by the Author G. Brookshaw.

«Le raisin peut bien sûr se manger frais, mais à quoi bon?» Cette phrase hérétique, que l'on entendra toujours énoncée sous une forme ou sous une autre par un amateur de vin convaincu – et dont on comprend parfaitement le sens – montre pourtant que notre disciple de Bacchus se prive à la légère d'un plaisir du palais. Ce n'est pas pour rien que la culture du raisin suit un objectif différent, selon qu'il est destiné au pressoir ou à la table. Pour le raisin à vin, seul compte le goût que le fruit communiquera à la boisson. Mais en ce qui concerne le raisin de table, l'œil et le palais ont tous deux leurs exigences: belle apparence, pépins aussi peu sensibles que possible, peau fine et bien sûr parfum adapté.

Revenons au raisin transformé en boisson. Depuis au moins 6000 ans, l'homme sait en tirer un jus dont le sucre produit une fermentation alcoolique en présence de levure. Les vins de l'époque avaient certainement un tout autre goût que celui auquel nous sommes habitués aujourd'hui, mais ils trouvaient manifestement beaucoup d'adeptes au Proche-Orient et en Egypte, et les Grecs aussi leur faisaient honneur. Leur vin résineux caractéristique, la retsina, est encore apprécié aujourd'hui. Avec les Romains, la culture de la vigne se répandit en Europe. Au Moyen Age, l'Eglise joua un rôle important. Car la parole de Jésus «Je suis le cep; vous êtes les sarments» (Jean 15,5) a donné à cette plante une signification symbolique particulière et explique que sa culture soit très répandue dans les couvents. L'extension de la vigne, telle que nous la connaissons aujourd'hui, ne commence toutefois qu'au XVIIIe siècle. Au XIXe siècle, elle connut un recul, avec l'arrivée du phylloxéra d'Amérique, qui menaça encore plus fortement les cultures que le mildiou, connu depuis longtemps. Les variétés américaines étaient certes immunisées contre ce parasite importun, mais le goût de leur vin ne pouvait pas satisfaire les viticulteurs et les amateurs allemands. Une astuce sortit tout le monde d'affaire: comme le phylloxéra ne s'attaquait qu'aux racines des pieds européens, on greffa les variétés recherchées sur des pieds américains immunisés. Grâce, notamment, à ces mesures défensives, d'innombrables variétés sont apparues depuis. Et pourvu qu'il s'en donne la peine, chacun trouvera toujours bouteille à «son» goût. Il n'est pas besoin, pour cela, de se limiter aux pays occidentaux traditionnels – Italie, Espagne, France ou Allemagne – car l'amateur découvrira aussi un grand choix de vins blancs, rosés ou rouges sur d'autres continents, de l'Afrique du Sud à l'Amérique, et ailleurs. C'est le procédé de fermentation qui détermine la couleur du vin. Ainsi, les vins blancs proviennent du moût d'un raisin vert ou blanc pressé, le rosé du jus de raisin rouge et le vin rouge de la masse pressée d'un raisin rouge ou noir, mis à fermenter avec les pellicules des fruits. Ce sont ces pellicules qui donnent la couleur rouge. Grâce aux nombreux éléments naturels qui le composent, le vin peut même être un remède délicieux s'il est consommé avec modération.

PLATE XLIX

Blue Muscadine Grape
Blauer Gutedel (Königs-Gutedel)
Chasselas violet

PLATE XLIX.

Blue Muscadine.

Painted & Pub. by the Author G. Brookshaw.

Painted & Pub. as the Act directs by H. G. Brookshaw.

PLATE. L.

Black Muscadine.

PLATE LII.

Engraved & Published as the Act directs by the Author, 1 November 1809.

Painted & Pub. as the Act directs, by H. G. Brookshaw.

PLATE LIII.

Muscat of Alexandria

PLATE LV.

Grizzly Frontinac.

Painted & Pub.d by the Author G. Brookshaw.

PLATE LVI.

Red Frontiniac.

Painted & Pub. by the Author G. Brookshaw.

PLATE LVII.

Black Frontiniac.

Painted & Pub. by the Author G. Brookshaw.

PLATE. LVIII.

West St. Peters.

GRAPE PRESERVE WITH MUSTARD, TURKISH STYLE

10–12 lbs white or blue grapes, mustard grains, mustard seeds

From ten to twelve pounds of white or blue grapes select the best and cut them into smaller clusters; separate out all the squashed and small grapes, squeeze out their juice, strain it through a hair-sieve, cook it for a few minutes in a very clean vessel and then allow it to cool. Carefully rinse the selected grapes in water and drain them thoroughly on a sieve. Then scatter a layer of mustard grains on the bottom of an earthen pot, lay some grapes on top, strew another layer of mustard seeds over these and continue to layer the grapes thus; finally pour the cooked grape juice over them, cover tightly and allow to stand for at least four to six weeks before use. In this way the grapes are preserved for a very long time and make a nice tangy condiment for roasts.

WEINBEEREN, EINZUMACHEN MIT SENF, AUF TÜRKISCHE ART

5–6 Kilogramm weißer oder blauer Trauben, Senfkörner, Senfsamen

Von 5–6 Kilogramm weißer oder blauer Trauben sucht man die besten heraus, zerschneidet sie in kleinere Träubchen, legt alle zerquetschten und kleinen Beeren bei Seite, preßt den Saft davon aus, seiht ihn durch ein Haarsieb, läßt ihn in einem sehr sauberen Gefäß einige Minuten kochen und dann auskühlen. Die ausgelesenen Trauben werden behutsam in Wasser abgespült und auf einem Sieb gehörig abgetropft. Dann streut man auf den Boden eines Steintopfes eine Schicht Senfkörner, legt etliche Trauben darauf, überstreut dieselben wiederum mit einer Prise Senfsamen und fährt so mit dem Einschichten der Trauben fort, die man zuletzt mit dem abgekochten Weinbeersaft übergießt, fest zubindet und mindestens 4–6 Wochen stehen läßt, bevor man sie in Gebrauch nimmt. Sie halten sich auf diese Art sehr lange und geben eine angenehm säuerliche Zukost zu dem gebratenen Fleisch.

CONSERVES DE RAISIN À LA MOUTARDE, À LA MANIÈRE TURQUE

5 à 6 kilogrammes de raisin noir ou blanc, graines de moutarde, semences de moutarde

Dans 5 à 6 kilogrammes de raisin noir ou blanc, sélectionnez les meilleures grappes et découpez-les en grappes plus petites. Mettez de côté tous les grains écrasés ou plus petits, pressez-en le jus, passez-le au tamis, faites-le cuire quelques minutes dans un récipient très propre puis laissez refroidir. Les grappes triées sont délicatement rincées à l'eau et égouttées dans une passoire. Parsemez le fond d'un pot en pierre de graines de moutarde et déposez-y quelques grappes. Saupoudrez de nouveau d'une pincée de semences de moutarde et continuez ainsi à superposer les grappes, couche après couche. A la fin, versez le jus de raisin cuit précédemment, fermez bien le couvercle et laissez reposer pendant au moins 4 à 6 semaines avant utilisation. De cette façon, le raisin se conserve très longtemps et accompagne d'un goût agréablement acide la viande rôtie.

PLATE LIX

Black Hamburgh Grape
Trollinger (Blauer Trollinger)
Grand noir

PLATE·LIX.

PLATE LX

White Hamburgh Grape

—

—

PLATE LX.

PLATE LXI.

Painted & Pub. by the Author G.Brookshaw.

PLATE LXII.
The Frankindale.

Designed & Etch by the Author G. Brookshaw

PLATE LXIII
Painted & Published as the Act directs by the Author G Brookshaw 1812

MELONS
Melonen | Melons

Although closely related to cucumbers, melons do not share their bitterness. Whether Muskmelon, Honeydew, or Netted Cantalope, all have a pleasant refreshing sweetness, even the less strongly flavoured Watermelon, which is botanically classed within another genus of the gourd family, originating from southern Central Africa, and was an early arrival to the Mediterranean region. *Citrullus*, the name it still carries today, probably derives from the Italian *citrullo*, meaning sap-head or dumbbell, mockingly drawing an analogy between these bloated giant fruits and the lack of substance of a simpleton's mind.

The Muskmelon, *Cucumis melo ssp. melo* L., and its varieties come from the Middle East and were likewise introduced early into the warmer climates of the Mediterranean, where they have been valued since olden days as a sweet thirst quencher and delicacy. Today melons are usually easily procured at markets even in the more temperate zones. The greater part of global production is from Asia, particularly China, Turkey and Iran, but the USA, Spain, Brazil and other countries are also important suppliers, and even some areas of Germany, such as, for instance, the Palatinate, Kraichgau and the southern Rhine valley, nurture the long trailers of these imposing fruits.

It is recommended to remove the dark seeds from the flesh before eating. The tough exteriors are not edible but offer attractive serving possibilities. Such attractive arrangements may have enticed Emperor Albrecht II (1397–1439) and Pope Paul II (reigned 1464–1471) to their rumored overindulgence, leading to their untimely deaths. But the tragic fate of these gourmets should not obscure the nutritional value of these fruits as a rich source of minerals and vitamins for a healthy diet.

PLATE LXIV

Scarlet Fleshed Romana Melon

—

—

PLATE LXIV.

Scarlet flesh Romana?

Painted & Pub. by the Author's Resolution.

Zwar gehört die Gurke zu ihren nahen Verwandten, aber den herben Geschmack hat die Melone nicht mit ihr gemeinsam. Gleichgültig ob Zucker-, Honig-, Netz- oder Kantalup-Melonen: Ein angenehm erfrischender und süßer Geschmack ist ihnen allen zu eigen, sogar − wenn auch etwas schwächer − der Wassermelone. Letztere gehört botanisch zu einer anderen Gattung der Kürbisgewächse, stammt ursprünglich aus dem südlichen Zentralafrika, gelangte aber schon früh ins Mittelmeergebiet. Ihr noch heute gültiger lateinischer Name *Citrullus* leitet sich wohl vom italienischen „citrullo", Dummkopf, ab und vergleicht spöttisch die aufgeblasenen, riesigen Früchte und ihrem wassertriefenden Inhalt mit dem vermeintlich ebenso substanzlosen Kopf eines einfältigen Menschen.

Die Zuckermelone, *Cucumis melo ssp. melo* L., und ihre Varietäten stammen aus dem mittelasiatischen Bereich und verbreiteten sich ebenfalls schon früh im warmen Klima der Mittelmeerländer, wo sie als süßer Durstlöscher und delikates Obst seit alters geschätzt werden. Aber auch auf den Märkten kühlerer Regionen ist die Melone heute meist leicht erhältlich. Der Großteil der Weltproduktion wird in Asien, insbesondere in China, der Türkei und dem Iran erzeugt, doch sind ebenso die USA, Spanien, Brasilien und andere Überseeländer wichtige Lieferanten, und sogar in einigen Gegenden Deutschlands, so zum Beispiel in der Pfalz, im Kraichgau und im südlichen Rheintal reifen die stattlichen Früchte an den langen Ranken.

Zum Verzehr empfiehlt es sich, die dunklen Samen aus dem Fruchtfleisch zu entfernen. Die harte Schale ist ungenießbar, eröffnet aber beim Anrichten attraktive Gestaltungsmöglichkeiten. Vielleicht war es ja eine solche verlockende Präsentation, die gemeinsam mit dem delikaten Geschmack dazu führte, dass Kaiser Albrecht II. (1397−1439) ebenso wie Papst Paul II. (reg. 1464−1471) den Zuckermelonen derart zusprachen, dass man munkelte, diese seien schuld an ihrem vorzeitigen Tod gewesen. Dennoch sollten diese tragischen Einzelschicksale zweier Feinschmecker nicht darüber hinwegtäuschen, dass Melonen wegen ihres Reichtums an Mineralstoffen und Vitaminen ein für die Ernährung wie für die Gesundheit wertvolles Obst sind.

PLATE LXV

White-seeded Rock Melon

—

—

PLATE LXV.

White Seedd Rock?

Proche parent du concombre, mais appartenant à une autre espèce de cucurbitacées, le melon n'en a pas le goût austère. Car quelle qu'en soit la variété – melon sucrin, melon d'eau, melon brodé ou cantaloup – il offre toujours un goût agréablement rafraîchissant et sucré, même quand il s'agit de pastèques, à la saveur moins prégnante. Originaire du sud de l'Afrique centrale, le melon d'eau s'est implanté tôt dans le bassin méditerranéen. Le nom latin de *citrullus* qu'on lui donne encore aujourd'hui provient probablement de l'italien « citrullo » (bêta en français). Sans doute ce fruit énorme et rond, gorgé d'eau, faisait-il penser à la tête d'un simple d'esprit, parfois grosse mais vide de substance.

Le melon sucrin, *cucumis melo ssp. melo* L. et ses variétés proviennent du Moyen-Orient et se sont tôt répandues sous le climat chaud du bassin méditerranéen où ce fruit délicat et suave étanche délicieusement la soif. Mais même dans les régions plus froides, le melon s'est aujourd'hui fait une place sur la plupart des marchés. La majeure partie de la production mondiale vient d'Asie, en particulier de Chine, de Turquie et d'Iran, mais aussi des Etats-Unis, d'Espagne, du Brésil et d'autres pays d'outre-mer, et même de certaines régions d'Allemagne, telles que le Palatinat, le Kraichgau et le sud de la vallée du Rhin où l'on peut voir mûrir ces gros fruits au bout de leurs longues vrilles.

Pour les consommer, il faut éliminer les graines sombres de la chair. La peau est dure et non comestible mais permet des présentations créatives. Peut-être sa saveur et sa présentation ont-elles tellement séduit l'empereur Albert II (1397–1439) et le pape Paul II (reg. 1464–1471) qu'on a pu imputer au melon sucrin la mort prématurée de ces deux personnalités. Mais ces destinées individuelles ne devraient pas faire oublier que grâce à sa forte teneur en minéraux et en vitamines, le melon reste un fruit précieux pour l'alimentation et la santé.

PLATE LXVI

Scarlet Flesh Rock Melon

PLATE 66.
Scarlet Flesh Rock.

Painted & Pub. by the Author at the Art. Street 1812.

PLATE LXVII

Silver Rock Melon

—

—

PLATE LXVIII (Page | Seite 148)

Polignac Melon

—

—

PLATE 67.

Silver Rock Melon.

Drawn & Pub. by the Author as the Act directs. 1812.

PLATE LXVIII.

PLATE LXIX.
Published as the Act directs by the Author & Ho of Shaw &c.

PLATE LXIX *(Page | Seite 149)*
Green flesh Melon
Grünfleischige Melone
—

PLATE LXX

Cantlope Melon
Kantalup-Melone
Melon de Florence

PLATE LIII

MELON ICE

1 ripe melon, 4 1/2 cups sugar, 1 1/2 pint water, 1/2 pint white wine,
1 lb refined sugar, juice of 2 or 3 lemons

Pare and cut up one fine, very ripe melon, remove the pulp and pound it in a mortar or grate it on a grater; for every pound of the grated fruit pulp, mix in a cooked syrup of four and a half cups sugar to a pint of water, strain and fill into the freezing tin. A half pint of fine white wine is often added to this fruit puree; strain this mixture through a hair-sieve, add one pound of refined sugar and the juice of two or three lemons, stir the mixture well and fill it into the freezing tin.

MELONEN-EIS

1 reife Melone, 375 Gramm Zucker, 3/4 Liter Wasser, 1/4 Liter Weißwein,
1/2 Kilogramm geläuterter Zucker, Saft von zwei bis drei Zitronen

Eine schöne, sehr reife Melone wird geschält, auseinandergeschnitten, von dem Mark befreit, im Mörser gestoßen oder auf dem Reibeisen gerieben, jedes 1/2 Kilogramm dieses Fruchtbreies mit einem aus 375 Gramm Zucker und 1/2 Liter Wasser gekochten Syrup vermischt, durchgestrichen und in die Gefrierbüchse gefüllt. Häufig mengt man den Fruchtbrei auch mit 1/4 Liter Wasser sowie 1/4 Liter feinem Weißwein, streicht dieses Gemisch durch ein Haarsieb, thut 1/2 Kilogramm geläuterten Zucker und den Saft von zwei bis drei Zitronen hinzu, rührt die Masse gut durcheinander und füllt sie in die Gefrierbüchse.

SORBET AU MELON

1 melon mûr, 375 grammes de sucre, 3/4 de litre d'eau, 1/4 de litre de vin blanc,
500 grammes de sucre raffiné, le jus de deux à trois citrons

Epluchez un beau melon bien mûr. Retirez les pépins, écrasez la chair du melon dans un mortier ou râpez-la, avant de la mélanger à du sirop obtenu en cuisant 375 grammes de sucre dans 1/2 litre d'eau pour 500 grammes de pulpe de fruit. Passez la préparation au tamis et versez-la dans la sorbetière. Variante : mélangez la purée de fruit à 1/4 de litre d'eau et 1/4 de litre de vin blanc fin, passez ce mélange au tamis, ajoutez 500 grammes de sucre raffiné, ainsi que le jus de deux à trois citrons, et mélangez bien la préparation avant de la verser dans la sorbetière.

PLATE LXXI

White Claudia (White Flesh Melon)

PLATE LXXI.

White Candia

Painted & Pub. by the Author, G.Brookshaw.

PLATE LXXII

Amicua Melon

—

—

PLATE LXXII.

Amicua

Painted & Pub. by the Author G.Brookshaw.

NUTS
Nüsse | Noisettes

In his *Historia naturalis* Pliny described the Hazelnut as the "Pontic nut", thus giving a clear indication of its origins in Asia Minor. From there it spread rapidly throughout Europe and made its way into our gardens during the Middle Ages, although for a long time it was gathered from bushes growing in the wild, which draw attention to themselves in the early spring with their yellow catkins. Although a pretty sight, it comes at the price of a bout of hayfever for those suffering from a pollen allergy. The twigs of the hazel bring us within the realm of myth and the esoteric, since a forked twig cut from a hazel bush was traditionally the preferred divining rod to detect all sorts of things, not just water. Besides the wild hazelnut varieties, only the nuts bred in the 16th century near Würzburg and Bamberg, the large Hazel or Cobnut and the little red Lambert (the name signals its Lombardian origins), play a role in today's marketplaces. At the end of the 18th century, the American Filbert was added to the European varieties and extensive crossing between all these related species resulted in the choice modern hybrids known since the 19th century. The fringed husk or cupula, which fully or partially envelops the nut on the bush, beckons one to "unwrap" and enjoy it either in the natural state, or roasted, or as a sweet or savoury sandwich spread.

In seiner *Historia naturalis* nennt Plinius die Haselnuss „Pontische Nuss" und gibt uns damit einen deutlichen Hinweis auf ihre ursprünglich kleinasiatische Herkunft. Schnell verbreitete sie sich aber über ganz Europa und fand im Mittelalter auch Eingang in die Gärten, wenngleich zum Verzehr noch lange die Früchte der wild wachsenden Sträucher gesammelt wurden, die schon im zeitigen Frühjahr durch ihre gelben Kätzchenblüten auffallen, den Blick auf ihre Schönheit aber vielen Heuschnupfenkranken durch die Pollenallergie verleiden. In den Bereich des Sagenumwobenen und ein wenig Esoterischen bringen uns dagegen die Zweige der Hasel, denn abgeschnittene Astgabeln dienen seit langem bevorzugt als Wünschelrute, um alles Mögliche, nicht nur Wasser, aufzuspüren. Neben den wildwachsenden Haselnüssen spielen auf dem Markt heute nur noch die im 16. Jahrhundert um Würzburg und Bamberg gezüchteten großen Zeller Nüsse sowie die nach ihrer Herkunft aus der Lombardei als Lambertnuss bezeichnete Art mit kleinen roten Nüssen eine Rolle. Am Ende des 18. Jahrhunderts kam zusätzlich noch die amerikanische Hasel nach Europa und durch vielfältige Kreuzung zwischen all diesen Verwandten selektierten die Züchter seit dem 19. Jahrhundert die heutigen Sorten. Die fransige Cupula, deren Nüsse am Strauch mehr oder weniger bedeckt sind, lädt förmlich zum „Auspacken" ein und der freigelegte Inhalt wird – naturbelassen, geröstet, zu süßem Brotaufstrich oder zu leckeren Süßigkeiten verarbeitet – den Genießer immer wieder zufrieden stellen.

Dans son *Histoire naturelle*, Pline appelle la noisette la « noix pontique », ce qui donne un indice sur sa terre d'origine, l'Asie mineure. Mais la noisette s'est vite répandue dans toute l'Europe où elle a fait son entrée dans les jardins dès le Moyen Age. Pour la consommation, on cueillit encore pendant longtemps le fruit des arbustes sauvages, qui tôt au printemps se signalent par leur floraison de chatons jaunes. Mais ceux que leur pollen rend allergique ou qui craignent le rhume des foins s'en écartent avec prudence. Avec la branche de noisetier, nous entrons dans le royaume des légendes et de l'ésotérisme, car une fourche coupée de cet arbre a longtemps servi de baguette de sourcier, pour rechercher de l'eau et toutes sortes d'autres choses. Outre la noisette sauvage, seules la grosse *noix de Zell* cultivée au XVIᵉ siècle dans la région de Wurtzbourg et de Bamberg et la noisette franche, plus petite et rouge, originaire de Lombardie, occupe encore aujourd'hui une place significative sur les marchés. A la fin du XVIIIᵉ siècle, leur cousine américaine se joint à cette petite famille et après de multiples croisements entre elles, les cultivateurs ont sélectionné à partir du XIXᵉ siècle les variétés d'aujourd'hui. La cupule frangée qui recouvre plus ou moins la noisette sur la branche incite à littéralement « déballer » son contenu qui, une fois libéré, peut être mangé nature, grillé, écrasé en pâte à tartiner sucrée, ou intégré à de délicieuses confiseries pour de multiples plaisirs gourmands.

PLATE LXXIII

White Filbert · Scarlet Filbert · Great Cob · Barcelona · Varieties · White Hazel Nut · Brown Hazel Nut

Weiße Lambertnuss · Rote Lambertnuss · Spanische Lambertnuss · Englische Zellernuss · Varietäten ·
Weiße Haselnuss · Braune Haselnuss

Aveline blanche · Aveline rouge · Noisetier d'Espagne · Barcelone · Variétés ·
Noisette blanche · Noisette brune

PLATE LXXIII

FIGS
Feigen | Figues

Botanists place the fig tree in the mulberry family. It is native to Caria, that part of the southwestern coast of Asia Minor off which the islands of Rhodes and Kos are located. The specific botanical name *Ficus carica* still reveals this origin. It has been grown there and in regions of western Asia for 5000 years for its sweet and very nutritious fruits. The tree and its fruits are mentioned many times in the Bible, often in connection with wine. At the latest around 700 B.C. the fig tree arrived in Greece, thence or via the Phoenicians to Italy, where the fig harvest is an important economic factor even today. The tree or bush with its large, hand-shaped, lobed leaves and pear-shaped green or dark red fruits can be found throughout the Mediterranean and many climatically amenable regions of Asia and North Africa. Figs are even cultivated along the German wine route. When the tree is injured, it secretes a white, latex-like milk that is very adhesive. It was noticed very early on that it causes milk to curdle, which is why people were advised not to drink milk after eating figs. A fig cheese is still made in Spain, as well as dessert wines and a coffee substitute. Most figs are eaten fresh or dried, however, and are intensely sweet treats, due to their high sugar content, but for this reason they also stimulate the digestion and have a laxative effect.

Botanisch gehört der Feigenbaum zu den Maulbeergewächsen. Seine Heimat hat er in der antiken Landschaft Karien, jenem Teil der Südwestküste Kleinasiens, dem die Inseln Rhodos und Kos vorgelagert sind. Im botanischen Namen *Ficus carica* kommt diese Herkunft noch heute zum Ausdruck. Seit etwa 5000 Jahren wird er wegen seiner süßen und sehr nahrhaften Früchte dort und im westasiatischen Bereich gezogen. In der Bibel werden Baum und Früchte mehrfach erwähnt, häufig zusammen mit dem Wein. Spätestens um 700 v. Chr. kam der Feigenbaum nach Griechenland und von dort oder über phönizische Vermittlung nach Italien, wo die Ernte seiner Früchte noch heute einen wichtigen Wirtschaftsfaktor ausmacht. Im gesamten Mittelmeergebiet und vielen klimatisch geeigneten Regionen Asiens und Nordafrikas findet sich der Baum oder Strauch mit seinen großen, handförmig gelappten Blättern und den birnförmigen grünen oder dunkelroten Früchten. Sogar an der Deutschen Weinstraße wird die Feige zur Fruchtreife gebracht. Bei Verletzungen des Baumes tritt ein weißer, latexartiger Milchsaft aus, der stark klebt. Schon früh hat man bemerkt, dass er Milch zur Gerinnung bringt, weshalb abgeraten wurde, nach dem Genuss von Feigen Milch zu trinken. In Spanien wird noch heute ein Feigenkäse hergestellt, aber auch Dessertweine und Feigenkaffe werden aus den Früchten gewonnen. Der Großteil wird jedoch frisch oder getrocknet gegessen und erfreut den Genießer wegen des hohen Zuckergehalts durch eine auffallende Süße, wirkt aus dem gleichen Grund aber auch verdauungsanregend und abführend.

Le figuier appartient à la famille des moracées. Il est né dans les paysages de l'antique Carie, région côtière du sud-ouest de l'Asie mineure, face aux iles de Rhodes et de Cos. Cette origine est restée inscrite dans son nom botanique, *ficus carica*. La culture de ce fruit sucré et nourrissant se pratique dans cette région ainsi qu'en Asie occidentale depuis environ 5000 ans. Dans la Bible, l'arbre et son fruit sont mentionnés à plusieurs reprises, souvent en rapport avec le vin. Vers 700 av. J.-C. au plus tard, le figuier s'implante en Grèce et de là, par l'intermédiaire des Phéniciens, en Italie, où son fruit alimente encore aujourd'hui un marché important. Arbre ou arbrisseau aux larges feuilles lobées en forme de main, il est, avec ses fruits piriformes verts ou rouge profond, une marque caractéristique du paysage méditerranéen et de nombreuses régions d'Asie et d'Afrique du Nord au climat ressemblant. Même en Allemagne, on voit mûrir la figue sur la route des vins. Une entaille dans l'arbre fait apparaître un jus blanc laiteux, extrêmement collant, semblable à du latex. L'homme ayant très tôt constaté que ce jus faisait cailler le lait, il a été déconseillé de boire du lait après avoir mangé des figues. Encore aujourd'hui, les Espagnols fabriquent un fromage, des vins de dessert et un café à base de ce fruit. Mais pour l'essentiel, les figues sont consommées fraiches ou séchées et réjouissent le gourmet par leur haute teneur en sucre, qui stimule la digestion et exerce un effet laxatif.

PLATE LXXIV

White Hanover · White Marseilles · Brown Naples · Purple Fig · Green Ischia · Brunswick

Weiße Hannover · Große Weiße Feige · Morellenfeige (Braune Neapolitanerin) · Birnenfeige · Grüne Ischia-Feige · Madonnenfeige (Braunschweiger Feige)

Hanovre blanc · Figue blanche · Fleur rouge · Figue poire · Ischia verte à longue queue · Brunswick

PLATE LXXIV
Painted & Published, as the Act directs by the Author G. Brookshaw 1807

FIG SOUP

4 1/2 oz dried figs, 2 1/4 oz fine semolina, 1 pinch of salt, some sugar,
a teaspoonful of orange-flower water

Chop four and a half ounces of fine dried figs into small pieces, cook them in one quart of boiling water for a quarter of an hour; beat two and a fourth ounces of fine semolina in cold water until smooth, stir it into the fig soup and keep it stirring as it cooks for a quarter of an hour; season with a pinch of salt, some sugar and a teaspoonful of orange-flower water and send this soup to table, which makes a quite excellent mild starter for sick persons with a fever.

FEIGEN-SUPPE

125 Gramm getrocknete Feigen, 62 Gramm feinen Gries, 1 Prise Salz,
etwas Zucker, einen Löffel Orangenblüthenwasser

125 Gramm schöne getrocknete Feigen schneidet man in kleine Stücke, läßt sie in 1 Liter siedendem Wasser eine Viertelstunde lang kochen, quirlt 62 Gramm feinen Gries in kaltem Wasser glatt, rührt ihn zu der Feigensuppe, läßt ihn unter fleißigem Umrühren eine Viertelstunde damit kochen, fügt eine Prise Salz, etwas Zucker und einen Löffel Orangenblüthenwasser hinzu und giebt die Suppe auf, welche als sanft eröffnendes Mittel für fiebernde Kranke ganz vortreffliche Dienste thut.

SOUPE DE FIGUES

125 grammes de figues séchées, 62 grammes de semoule fine,
1 pincée de sel, un peu de sucre, eau de fleur d'oranger

Coupez en petits morceaux 125 grammes de belles figues séchées. Faites-les cuire pendant un quart d'heure dans de l'eau bouillante. Mouillez 62 grammes de semoule fine avec de l'eau froide, ajoutez la semoule à la soupe de figues, laissez cuire pendant un quart d'heure en emuant activement, ajoutez une pincée de sel, un peu de sucre et une cuillerée d'eau de fleur d'oranger, et servez cette soupe qui ravigote en douceur les malades atteints de fièvre.

PLATE LXXV

Green Ischia · Red Turkey Fig · Earl of Besborary · — · Brown Malta · Black Ischia

Grüne Ischia-Feige · Rote Türkische Feige · Graf von Besborary · —
Gemeine runde Feige (Braune Malteser Feige) · Schwarze Ischia-Feige

Ischia verte à longue queue · Figue rouge de Turquie · — · — · Malta brune · Ischia noire

PEARS
Birnen | Poires

Homer mentioned pears in his *Odyssey* and Pliny, of course, described them in his monumental *Historia naturalis*, where we are not only introduced by name to many different varieties, but also learn that it was considered the fruit of the goddess of love, Venus. With such bright white blossoms and crimson stamens, who would be surprised? Pears were cultivated in the Mediterranean for around 3000 years. But they originate from western Asia and became known to the Greeks and Romans from Asia Minor, who soon preferred them to the native wild varieties. Those small and hard fruits are graphically described in German as "woody" (*Holzbirne*) and are only edible after cooking. Most of the modern hybrids are noted for their "buttery"-textured, juicy flesh that gives off a characteristic, fine aroma at room temperature. These varieties were developed in the mid-18th century and French, Belgian and German crosses have become particularly popular. Around 1770 the Williams' Bon Chrétien pear was bred in England and has since become the most important variety today in the canning industry (known in America as the Bartlett).

Most varieties are picked before they have reached full maturity and only ripen in storage under suitable conditions. But once fully ripe they do not keep long and should be consumed as soon as possible. The hard grains often found in the flesh are not a sign of bad quality but are grit cells typical of the species. They make pears less digestible for many people than apples, however, which are otherwise nutritionally very similar.

The cultivated varieties cannot be propagated from seed, but only asexually. A twig, or scion, is grafted onto a suitable understock, often the stem of a quince, which supplies it with water and nutrients, allowing it to develop gradually in the following years into a fruit-bearing pear tree. "Graft the pear trees, Daphnis", Virgil wrote in his ninth pastoral poem, "the grandchildren shall pick the fruits!", alluding to the patience demanded of a gardener but also the joys reaped from foresight.

PLATE LXXVI

Petit Muscat (Early Muscat Pear) · Green Sugar Pear · Green Chisel Pear · Citron de Charmes · —
Kleine Muskateller (Sieben ins Maul) · Grüne Herbstzuckerbirne · Schnabelsbirne · Grüne Sommer-Magdalene · —
Sept en gueule · Sucré vert · Guinette · Citron de Charmes (Poire de Madeleine) · —

PLATE LXXVI.

Homer erwähnt die Birne in seiner *Odyssee* und natürlich findet sie sich auch in der monumentalen *Historia naturalis* des Plinius beschrieben, wo wir nicht nur eine große Zahl unterschiedlicher Sorten namentlich kennen lernen, sondern auch erfahren, dass sie als Frucht der Liebesgöttin Venus galt. Wen wundert's bei den leuchtend weißen Blütenblätter und den roten Staubgefäßen? Seit etwa dreitausend Jahren wird die Birne im Mittelmeerraum kultiviert, stammt ursprünglich jedoch aus Westasien und wurde über Kleinasien den Griechen und Römern bekannt, die sie schnell den einheimischen Wildsorten vorzogen. Ihre kleinen und harten Früchte werden „Holzbirne" genannt und sind allenfalls gekocht genießbar. Dagegen zeichnen sich die meisten der neuzeitlichen Züchtungen durch weich schmelzendes Fruchtfleisch aus, das sehr viel Saft führt und bei Zimmertemperatur das charakteristische feine Aroma entfaltet. Sie bildeten sich seit der Mitte des 18. Jahrhunderts heraus, wobei sich insbesondere französische und belgische, aber auch deutsche Züchtungen großer Beliebtheit erfreuten. Aus England kam um 1770 die Williams-Christ-Birne, die heute in der Konservenindustrie die größte Bedeutung besitzt.

Bei den meisten Sorten werden die Früchte bereits vor der völligen Reife gepflückt, die sie erst bei entsprechender Lagerung, der so genannten Nachreife, erreichen. Dann jedoch sind sie nur noch begrenzt haltbar und sollten baldmöglichst verzehrt werden. Die im Fruchtfleisch häufig wahrnehmbaren harten Körnchen stellen keinen Qualitätsmangel dar, sondern sind arttypische verholzte Zellen, die allerdings dazu führen, dass Birnen für viele Menschen schwerer verdaubar sind als Äpfel, denen sie ansonsten im Nährwert und im Spektrum der Inhaltsstoffe sehr nahe kommen.

Die Kultursorten können nicht durch Samen, sondern nur ungeschlechtlich vermehrt werden. Hierzu pfropft man einen Zweig, das so genannte Edelreis, auf eine geeignete Unterlage, häufig den Stamm einer Quitte, die ihn mit Wasser und Nährstoffen versorgt, so dass er sich in den Folgejahren langsam zum Frucht tragenden Birnbaum entwickeln kann. „Pfropfe die Birnbäume, Daphnis, die Enkel pflücken die Früchte!" schreibt Vergil im neunten seiner Hirtengedichte und spielt damit auf die Geduld an, die vom Gärtner verlangt wird, aber auch auf seine vorausschauende Freude.

PLATE LXXVII

King Catherine Pear (Catherine Royal) · Lemon Pear · Late Petite Muscat · Oignon La Reine · Long stalked Blanquet
Catharinenbirne · Limonenförmige Birne · Grüne Muskateller (Chassolet) · Große Zwiebelbirne · Langstielige Blankette
Catherine royale · — · Poire muscat verte · Gros oignonet · Blanquet à longue queue

PLATE LXVII
Painted & Publish'd as the Act directs by the Author G Brookshaw Esq.

Homer évoque la poire dans son *Odyssée* et on la trouve bien sûr mentionnée dans la vaste *Historia naturalis* de Pline qui en décrit un grand nombre de variétés et nous apprend qu'elle était considérée comme le fruit de Vénus, déesse de l'amour. On ne s'en étonnera pas à la vue de ses fleurs blanches et lumineuses et de ses étamines rouges. La poire est cultivée depuis environ 3000 ans dans le bassin méditerranéen mais provient d'Asie occidentale. Les Grecs et les Romains la découvrirent en Asie mineure et la préférèrent bientôt aux variétés sauvages de leurs contrées, dont les fruits petits et durs sont appelés « poires des bois » en allemand et qui peuvent se manger cuits. En revanche, la plupart des variétés plus récentes se distinguent par leur chair fondante, très juteuse, et dégagent un arôme caractéristique à température ambiante. La plupart ont été développées à partir du milieu du XVIIIᵉ siècle, les variétés françaises et belges mais aussi allemandes ayant eu le plus grand succès. L'Angleterre a donné naissance vers 1770 à la poire Williams, la plus employée aujourd'hui dans l'industrie de la conserve.

Dans la plupart des variétés, la poire est cueillie avant maturité complète, qu'elle n'atteint qu'après un temps de stockage. Mais une fois mûre, elle doit être consommée rapidement car sa durée de conservation est limitée. Les grains durs que l'on trouve souvent dans sa chair ne dénotent pas un défaut de qualité mais sont des cellules scléreuses, caractéristiques de l'espèce. Cette propriété rend ce fruit moins digeste que la pomme, alors qu'il présente par ailleurs une valeur nutritive et un éventail d'éléments très proches.

Les variétés cultivées ne se reproduisent pas à partir des pépins mais uniquement de manière asexuée. A cet effet, on greffe une branche sur un support approprié, souvent le tronc d'un cognassier, qui alimente le greffon en eau et en substances nutritives jusqu'à ce qu'il devienne en quelques années un poirier capable de donner des fruits. « Greffe les poiriers, Daphnis, les petits enfants en récolteront les fruits ! », écrit Virgile dans la neuvième de ses *Buccoliques*, en faisant allusion à la patience du jardinier mais aussi à sa joie de planter pour l'avenir.

PLATE LXXVIII

PLATE LXXX *(Page | Seite 169)*
Chaumontelle Pear · Windsor Pear · Summer Bon Chretien
Wildling von Chaumontel · Römische Schmalzbirne · Sommer-Apothekerbirne
Besy de Chaumontel · Poire Madame · Bon Chrétien d'été

PLATE LXXXI

Double Blossom Pear · Swan's Egg Pear · Winter Swan's Egg Pear
Doppelt tragende Birne (Zweiträchtige) · Schwanenei-Birne · —
Double fleur · — · —

PLATE LXXXI.

PEAR DUMPLINGS

Fine pears, grated breadcrumb, 1 cupful milk, 2 or 3 eggs,
a few spoonsful of flour, sugar and cinnamon, cream sauce

Pare some fine pears and cut into cubes, mix together with grated breadcrumb, one cupful of milk, two or three eggs and a few spoonsful of flour; then scoop out the batter with a spoon and drop the dumplings into boiling water till cooked, dust them with sugar and cinnamon, and serve them as a sweet with a cream sauce.

BIRNEN-KLÖSSE

Gute Birnen, geriebene Semmel, Obertasse voll Milch,
2 bis 3 Eier, einige Löffel Mehl, Zucker und Zimt, Rahmsauce

Gute Birnen werden geschält, in Würfel geschnitten, mit geriebener Semmel, einer Obertasse voll Milch, zwei bis drei Eiern und einigen Löffeln voll Mehl vermischt, dann sticht man mit dem Löffel Klöße von dem Teig ab, kocht sie in Wasser, bestreut sie mit Zucker und Zimt und serviert sie mit einer Rahmsauce als Mehlspeiße.

BOULETTES AUX POIRES

De bonnes poires, chapelure, une tasse pleine de lait,
2 à 3 œufs, quelques cuillerées de farine, sucre et cannelle, sauce à la crème

Epluchez de bonnes poires et coupez-les en dés. Ajoutez une tasse de lait, deux à trois œufs, la chapelure et quelques cuillerées de farine. Mélangez bien. A l'aide de la cuillère, formez des boulettes dans la pâte ainsi obtenue, mettez-les à cuire dans de l'eau bouillante, saupoudrez de sucre et de cannelle et servez en entremets avec une sauce à la crème.

PLATE LXXXII

Brown Beurré · Golden Beurré (Pear) · Colmar Pear
Graue Herbstbutterbirne (Braune Butterbirne) · Goldbirne aus Bilbao · Colmar (Mannabirne)
Bayenne gris (Beurré gris) · Golden Beurré (Bilbao) · Poire de Colmar

PLATE LXXII
Painted & Published at the Art directs by the Author G. Brookshaw 1817

PLATE LXXXIII

Crassane Pear · Summer Bergamot · Orange Bergamot · —
Crassane · Große Sommer-Bergamotte · Orange Sommer-Bergamotte · —
Bergamote Crassane · Bergamote d'été · — · —

PLATE LXXXIV (Page | Seite 176)

Virgouleuse · Striped Vert Longue · — · Pear d'Auch
Virguleuse · Schweizerhose · — · Winter-Apothekerbirne von Auch
Poire de Virgouleuse · Bergamote suisse longue · — · Bon Chrétien d'hiver Auch

PLATE LXXXIII
Painted & Published as the Act directs by the Author & Brookshaw 1807

PLATE LXXXV
Painted & Published as the Act directs by the Author G Brookshaw 1807

PLATE LXXXVI
Painted & Published at the Act directs by the Author G. Brookshaw 1807

APPLES
Äpfel | Pommes

The grand entrance of the apple was, without a doubt, in Eden, although it is not even explicitly named in the Bible. Only "fruits" are mentioned there, and in particular that forbidden fruit from the tree of the knowledge "of good and evil", *bonum et malum*, as it reads in the Vulgate. But since the Latin *malum* can mean either "evil" or "apple", the conceptual link between the two terms was more than suggestive. Countless works of art refer back to it, and the Adam's apple, that neck prominence particularly noticeable on some men, is a living reminder of the fateful bite of fruit that became lodged in the throat of the first man. Apples have in fact accompanied mankind since time immemorial. Wild varieties with very small fruits were initially gathered, and around 5000 years ago cultivation gradually began in the Near East. The first crossbreedings opened the way to ever tastier and prettier fruits. Various apple varieties have come down to us from the Middle Ages, but true cultivation began only in the 16th century and was so successful from the 18th century onward that we now know of more than 20,000 different apple varieties.

Botanically, apple trees, like so many other fruit-bearing plants, belong to the rose family. After pollination, the base of the five-petalled blossoms grows around the carpel to develop into the soft succulent flesh surrounding the seed-carrying core. Besides fruit acids, sugars, and carbohydrates, apples contain numerous minerals and vitamins, which make them as nutritious as they are tasty. Even if the old adage "An apple a day keeps the doctor away" should not be taken too literally, apples ought not to be missing from our diets. The large numbers of recipes for cider or stewed fruit, jellies and baked apples all prove that apples have not yet lost their allure even among gourmets and no penalty or flaming sword is attached to relishing them.

PLATE LXXXVII

Pomme d'Api · Carpendu de Blanch · Carpendu de Rouge · Nonsuch Apple Royal · Nonsuch Summer · Margill
Kleiner Api · Weißer Kurzstiel · Königlicher Kurzstiel (Roter Kurzstiel) · Königlicher Sondergleichen · Früher Nonpareil (Wicks Liebling) · Muskatrenette
Pomme d'Api · Court-pendu blanc · Court-pendu rouge · Non-pareille royale · Non-pareille d'été · Reinette muscate

PLATE LXXXVII

Seinen großen Auftritt hatte der Apfel zweifellos im Paradies, auch wenn er in der Bibel gar nicht erwähnt wird. Lediglich von „Früchten" ist dort die Rede und ganz besonders von jener verbotenen Frucht, die erkennen lasse, was „gut und böse ist" − „bonum et malum", wie es in der lateinischen Vulgata heißt. Da aber im Lateinischen „malum" sowohl „das Böse" als auch „Apfel" bedeuten kann, lag die gedankliche Verbindung beider Begriffe mehr als nahe. Unzählige künstlerische Darstellungen greifen durch die Jahrhunderte darauf zurück und der Adamsapfel, der bei manchen Männern am Hals sehr deutlich hervortritt, erinnert uns mit seinem Namen noch heute an jenes abgebissene Stückchen Obst, das dem ersten Menschen in der Kehle stecken blieb. Tatsächlich begleiten Äpfel den Weg der Menschen schon seit unvordenklichen Zeiten. Anfangs wurden Wildsorten mit sehr kleinen Früchten gesammelt, dann begann vor etwa 5000 Jahren im vorderasiatischen Raum nach und nach die Kultivierung, und so kam man über erste Kreuzungen zu immer wohlschmeckenderen und ansehnlicheren Früchten. Aus dem Mittelalter sind uns zwar verschiedene Apfelsorten namentlich überliefert, aber die eigentliche Kultur beginnt erst im 16. Jahrhundert und erreicht seit dem 18. Jahrhundert derartige Erfolge, dass wir heute mehr als 20.000 verschiedene Apfelsorten kennen.

Botanisch gehört der Apfelbaum wie so viele andere Obst liefernde Pflanzen zu den Rosengewächsen. Der Boden der fünfzähligen Blüten umwächst nach der Bestäubung die Fruchtblätter und bildet dabei das saftige, weich werdende Fruchtfleisch, das das Kernhaus mit den Samen umgibt. Neben Fruchtsäuren, Zuckern und Kohlehydraten finden sich auch zahlreiche Mineralstoffe und Vitamine im Apfel, die ihn zu einem ebenso wohlschmeckenden wie wertvollen Nahrungsmittel machen. Wenn auch das alte englische Sprichwort „An apple a day keeps the doctor away" nicht ganz wörtlich zu nehmen ist, sollten Äpfel auf unserem Speiseplan nicht fehlen. Rezepte für ihre Zubereitung vom Apfelwein über das Kompott bis hin zu Gelee und Bratapfel gibt es in sehr großer Zahl und sie alle beweisen, dass der Apfel seine Verführungskraft nicht eingebüßt hat, nur gilt sie heute den Gourmets und der genüssliche Verzehr ist mit keinerlei Strafandrohung oder Flammenschwert versehen.

PLATE LXXXVIII

Rennet Grey · — · Bigg's Nonsuch · July-flower Apple (Cornish July-flower, Cornish Gilliflower) · Scarlet Pearmain · Ribston Peppin

Graue französische Renette · — · Biggs Sondergleichen · Cornwalliser Nelkenapfel · Englische Scharlachrote Parmäne · Ribston Pepping

Reinette grise · — · Non-pareille de Biggs · Calville d'Angleterre · Ecarlate d'été · Ribston Pippin

PLATE LXXXIII.

C'est évidemment par la porte du paradis que la pomme réalise sa grande entrée en scène. Pourtant, elle n'est nullement mentionnée dans la Bible. Il y est seulement question de fruits, et notamment du fruit interdit, qui permet de distinguer entre le Bien et le Mal – «bonum et malum», lit-on dans la Vulgate latine. Or comme en latin «malum» veut dire «le mal» mais aussi la «pomme», l'association entre ces deux notions s'est faite tout naturellement. D'innombrables représentations artistiques y font allusion au cours des siècles et la pomme d'Adam, qui est très proéminente chez certains hommes, nous rappelle par son nom la petite bouchée de ce fruit restée en travers de la gorge du premier être humain. Il est vrai que la pomme est l'amie de l'homme depuis la nuit des temps. Cueillie au départ à l'état sauvage, sous forme de très petits fruits, elle commence à être cultivée il y a environ 5000 ans en Asie mineure pour devenir progressivement, par croisements successifs, un fruit de plus en plus délicieux et de belle apparence. Différents noms de variétés utilisées au Moyen Age nous ont été transmis, mais la culture proprement dite de la pomme commence véritablement au XVIᵉ siècle et emporte de tels succès depuis le XVIIIᵉ siècle que nous connaissons aujourd'hui plus de 20 000 variétés de pommes différentes.

D'un point de vue botanique, le pommier fait partie, comme tant d'autres arbres fruitiers, de la famille des rosacées. Après la pollinisation, le fond des fleurs à cinq pétales pousse autour des étamines en donnant naissance à une chair tendre et juteuse qui entoure le trognon et ses pépins. La pomme contient des acides, des sucres, des glucides ainsi que de nombreux sels minéraux et vitamines qui font d'elle un aliment précieux et savoureux. Même s'il ne faut pas prendre entièrement à la lettre le vieux dicton anglais «An apple a day keeps the doctor away» (une pomme chaque jour tient éloigné le médecin), ce fruit ne devrait pas manquer dans notre régime alimentaire. Il existe de très nombreuses recettes pour toutes sortes de préparations, du cidre à la compote, en passant par la gelée et la pomme au four. Elles montrent toutes que la pomme n'a pas perdu de son pouvoir de séduction. Avec cette différence, toutefois, qu'elle s'adresse aujourd'hui au gourmet, et que la jouissance de sa chair n'est plus assortie d'aucun châtiment, ni de la menace d'une épée flamboyante.

PLATE LXXXIX
Painted & Published as the Act directs by the Author G Brookshaw 1807

APPLE PANCAKES

1 pint milk or cream, 4 eggs, dash of salt, 1 cup flour,
4–6 apples diced, 3 1/2 oz sugar, 4 heaped tablespoons butter

Beat the yolks of four eggs into one pint of milk or cream with a dash of salt and a generous cup of flour; add four to six diced apples and three and a half ounces of sugar to the mixture; pour the batter about three fingers deep into a skillet or frying pan containing four tablespoonsful of hot melted butter, cover it and place it in the upper oven for a quarter of an hour, after which remove the lid, allow the pancake to brown nicely on both sides and break it apart into large chunks with a fork.

APFEL-SCHMARRN

1/2 Liter Milch oder Rahm, 4 Eier, etwas Salz, 1/4 Liter Mehl,
4–6 würfliggeschnittene Äpfel, 100 Gramm Zucker, 60 Gramm Butter

Ein halber Liter Milch oder Rahm wird mit vier Eidottern, etwas Salz und reichlich 1/4 Liter Mehl gut zerquirlt, dazu mischt man vier bis sechs würfliggeschnittene Äpfel und 100 Gramm Zucker, gießt die Masse etwa drei Finger hoch in ein Kasserol oder eine Pfanne mit 60 Gramm kochender Butter, deckt dieselbe zu und stellt sie eine Viertelstunde in die obere Röhre, worauf man den Deckel abnimmt, den Schmarrn auf beiden Seiten schön braun bäckt und dann mit der Gabel in große Brocken zerreißt.

SCHMARRN AUX POMMES

1/2 litre de lait ou de crème liquide, 4 œufs, un peu de sel, 1 tasse de farine,
4 à 6 pommes coupées en dés, 100 grammes de sucre, 60 grammes de beurre

Mélangez, en remuant bien, un demi-litre de lait ou de crème liquide avec 4 jaunes d'œufs, un peu de sel et une belle tasse de farine bien pesée. Incorporez quatre à six pommes coupées en dés et 100 grammes de sucre. Versez trois doigts de la préparation dans un fait-tout ou une poêle. Ajoutez 60 grammes de beurre. Recouvrez la préparation et placez-la pendant un quart d'heure dans le haut du four, puis ôtez le couvercle. Quand vous aurez bien fait dorer le Schmarrn des deux côtés, déchirez-le en gros morceaux à l'aide d'une fourchette.

PLATE XC

Striped Holland Pippin · Marygold Apple · Sullenworth's Rennet Apple · — · — · Beauty of Kent
Goldrenette (Große Kassler Renette) · Marygold · Sullenworths Renette · — · — · Schöner aus Kent
Princesse noble · Marygold · Reinette de Sullenworth · — · — · Beauté de Kent

PLATE XC
Painted & Published as the Act directs by the Author G Brookshaw 1817

PLATE XCI.
Painted & Published as the Act directs by the Author G. Brookshaw, 1808.

PLATE XCIII.
Drawn & Published as the Act Directs, by the Author, Brook Taylor 1817.

POMONA BRITANNICA
From England to Greiz | Von England nach Greiz | De l'Angleterre à Greiz

The present reprint of the *Pomona Britannica*, an English guide to fruits, is based on the copy in the Staatliche Bücher- und Kupferstichsammlung /Stiftung der älteren Linie des Hauses Reuss, in Greiz, Thuringia. This high-quality original edition dating from 1812 in imperial folio format (78 x 57 cm) was a part of a very limited edition issued by the publishers' consortium of Whyte, Cochrane & Co., Fleet Street; E. Lloyd, Harley Street; and W. Lindell, Corner of Wigmore Street. The same care as was lavished on the production of the aquatint sheets also went into the printing of the text pages on wove paper of the highest quality. The text was typeset at a leading London establishment on Fleet Street by the renowned master printer Thomas Bensley. The typeface used was Didot Antiqua.

The Greiz copy is bound in brown morocco leather, with the letter E stamped on the front cover as an ex libris. The monogram is that of the book's original owner, one of the daughters of George III, king of England: Princess Elizabeth was the duchess of Brunswick-Lüneburg and later landgravine of Hesse-Homburg. The author of the book of fruits, George Brookshaw, dedicated his work to "His Royal Highness George, Prince Regent of the United Kingdom of Great Britain and Ireland". This brother of Elizabeth, who later acceded to the throne as George IV, was doubtless a patron of the work.

What do we know about the first owner of this book? What were her interests and preferences as a scholar, artist and passionate collector? Princess Elizabeth was the third daughter and seventh child of George III and his queen, Charlotte, princess of Mecklenburg-Strelitz. She was born in 1770 at Queen's House in London. Together with her brothers and sisters, she received a thorough education and artistic training.

Elizabeth had certain representative duties at court and devoted herself in particular to the visual arts, for which she had a particular talent. This is well-documented by her papers, which have survived in the collection of books and copperplate engravings at Greiz, along with substantial parts of her own collections. Among the thousands of copperplate engravings at the museum in Greiz, there are large numbers of exceptional mezzotint prints, for example.

The fame of Princess Elizabeth's historical, scientific, literary and artistic studies reached beyond England's shores even during her lifetime. After her marriage to the crown prince of Hesse-Homburg in 1818, the English princess's extraordinary collections, scientific and artistic studies and art treasures accompanied her to Germany.

So how did Princess Elizabeth acquire her copy of the *Pomona Britannica*, a work explicitly dedicated to her brother George? The exact train of events cannot be reconstructed any more. But many scenarios are conceivable. If she did not receive the book as a personal gift from Brookshaw, she may even have asked him for a copy. Perhaps the volume had been intended for her brother or for her father's royal library.

Be that as it may, there is much to be said for the possibility that, like numerous other works of art and presentation copies, this volume was a well-chosen gift for the artistically minded and scientifically educated princess. Elizabeth had begun to build the basis of her collections towards the close of the 18th century at Windsor Castle, but it was only from 1812 that she had an allowance for private book and art purchases.

Der vorliegende Reprint des englischen Früchtebuches *Pomona Britannica* beruht auf der in der Staatlichen Bücher- und Kupferstichsammlung zu Greiz/Thüringen, Stiftung der Älteren Linie des Hauses Reuss, verwahrten und besonders qualitätvollen Originalausgabe im Imperialfolio (78 x 57 cm) aus dem Jahre 1812. Dieses Exemplar, aus einer recht kleinen Auflage, erschien im Verlagskonsortium von Whyte, Cochrane & Co., Fleet Street / E. Lloyd, Harley Street / W. Lindell, Corner of Wigmore Street. Wie die Aquatintablätter, so sind auch die Texte mit großer Sorgfalt auf bestem Velinpapier von hoher Qualität gedruckt. Sämtliche Schriftblätter wurden in einer führenden Londoner Offizin in der Fleet Street durch den namhaften Drucker Thomas Bensley meisterhaft in der Didot'schen Antiqua gesetzt.

Das Greizer Exemplar ist in braunes Maroquinleder gebunden und trägt auf dem vorderen Einbanddeckel ein geprägtes Super-Exlibris mit dem Buchstaben „E". Das Monogramm verweist als Bucheignerzeichen auf die Prinzessin Elizabeth, Tochter des englischen Königs George III., Herzogin von Braunschweig-Lüneburg und spätere Landgräfin von Hessen-Homburg. Der Autor des Früchtebuches, George Brookshaw, widmete sein Werk dem Bruder von Elizabeth, „His Royal Highness George, Prince Regent of the United Kingdom of Great Britain and Ireland", nachfolgender König George IV., der sicherlich hier auch als Gönner hervorgetreten ist.

Was wissen wir über die Biografie, die geistig-künstlerischen Vorlieben und die Sammelleidenschaft der ersten Besitzerin dieses Buches? Prinzessin Eizabeth wurde 1770 als dritte Tochter und siebtes Kind von George III. und seiner Gemahlin, Königin Charlotte, geborene Prinzessin von Mecklenburg-Strelitz, geboren. Zusammen mit ihren Geschwistern erhielt sie eine fundierte wissenschaftliche Bildung und musische Erziehung. Elizabeth hatte am königlichen Hofe auch repräsentierende Pflichten zu erfüllen und widmete sich auf Grund der ihr eigenen musischen Talente insbesondere den bildenden Künsten. Ihr heute in der Bücher- und Kupferstichsammlung Greiz aufbewahrter schriftlicher Nachlass sowie umfangreiche Teile ihrer Sammlungen bestätigen dies. Unter den Tausenden von Kupferstichen im Greizer Museum ist beispielsweise eine große Anzahl von Schabkunstblättern in hervorragenden Abdrucken zu nennen.

Die historischen und wissenschaftlichen, literarischen und künstlerischen Studien der Prinzessin Elizabeth waren schon zu ihren Lebzeiten über die Grenzen Englands hinaus bekannt geworden. Durch ihre Heirat im Jahre 1818 mit dem Erbprinzen von Hessen-Homburg gelangte ihre außergewöhnliche Sammlung, wissenschaftlich-künstlerischer Arbeiten und Kunstschätze schließlich nach Deutschland.

Wie ist nun Prinzessin Elizabeth in den Besitz ihres Exemplars der *Pomona Britannica* gelangt, das ausdrücklich ihrem Bruder George gewidmet war? Der genaue Vorgang ist nicht mehr nachweisbar. Hier gibt es mehrere denkbare Möglichkeiten. Vielleicht hat sie das Buch persönlich von Brookshaw geschenkt bekommen oder sich sogar von ihm erbeten, vielleicht ist es aber auch das Exemplar des Bruders oder der königlichen Bibliothek, das ihrem Vater zugedacht war.

Vieles spricht dafür, dass dieses Buch, wie zahlreiche andere Kunstwerke und Widmungsexemplare, ein willkommenes Geschenk an die

La présente réimpression du livre de fruits anglais, *Pomona Britannica*, a été réalisée à partir d'un exemplaire original de très grande qualité, au format in-folio impérial (78 x 57 cm), datant de l'année 1812, et conservé dans la collection nationale de livres et d'estampes de la ville de Greiz (Thuringe, Allemagne). Provenant d'un don de la branche aînée de la maison Reuss, il faisait partie d'un tirage très limité, réalisé par le consortium d'éditeurs anglais Whyte, Cochrane & Co., Fleet Street / E. Lloyd, Harley Street / W. Lindell, Corner of Wigmore Street. Les aquatintes ainsi que le texte sont imprimés avec beaucoup de soin sur un vélin de grande qualité. La composition en Antiqua de Didot, réalisée de main de maître, est l'œuvre de l'un des plus grands imprimeurs de Londres, le célèbre Thomas Bensley.

Relié en maroquin brun, l'exemplaire de Greiz présente sur la première de couverture un superbe ex-libris imprimé, constitué de la lettre « E ». Ce monogramme est celui du propriétaire de l'ouvrage, la princesse Elisabeth, fille du roi George III d'Angleterre, duchesse de Brunswick-Lunebourg et ultérieurement landgrave de Hesse-Hombourg. George Brookshaw, auteur de cet ouvrage pomologique, dédia son œuvre au frère d'Elisabeth, « His Royal Highness George, Prince Regent of The United Kingdom of Great Britain and Ireland » (« Son Altesse Royale George, prince régent du Royaume Uni et d'Irlande »), le futur roi George IV.

Que savons-nous de la biographie, des goûts artistiques et de la passion de collectionneur d'Elisabeth, première propriétaire de ce livre ? La princesse née en 1770 est la troisième fille et le septième enfant du roi George III et de son épouse, la reine Charlotte, née princesse de Mecklembourg-Strelitz. Comme ses frères et sœurs, elle reçut une solide éducation scientifique et musicale.

A la Cour, Elisabeth avait certes à remplir des tâches de représentation mais son don pour la musique lui permit de se consacrer plus spécifiquement aux arts plastiques. C'est ce qu'attestent de nombreuses pièces de sa collection ainsi que les écrits de sa succession, conservés avec les livres et estampes de la ville de Greiz. Parmi les milliers de gravures sur cuivre que possède le musée de Greiz, il convient de citer le grand nombre de feuilles gravées à la manière noire (mezzotinto), d'une excellente qualité d'impression.

Les études historiques, scientifiques, littéraires et artistiques de la princesse étaient déjà connues de son temps au-delà des frontières de son pays. Lorsqu'Elisabeth fut mariée en 1818 au prince héritier de Hesse-Hombourg, les collections exceptionnelles, les travaux scientifiques et artistiques ainsi que les trésors d'art de cette princesse anglaise prirent la direction de l'Allemagne.

Mais comment la princesse était-elle entrée en possession de son exemplaire de la *Pomona Britannica*, qui avait été clairement dédié à son frère George ? Il n'est plus possible, aujourd'hui, d'en retracer les circonstances précises. Plusieurs hypothèses se présentent néanmoins à l'esprit. Peut-être Brookshaw lui avait-il offert personnellement l'ouvrage, ou le lui avait-elle demandé, à moins que cet exemplaire ne soit celui de son frère, ou de la bibliothèque royale, auquel cas il aurait initialement été destiné à son père.

Il semble à divers égards que cet ouvrage ait été, comme bien d'autres œuvres d'art et livres dédiés, un cadeau bienvenu pour une prin-

Summer Palace in Greiz, view from the west, before 1799
Unknown artist

Sommerpalais Greiz, Ansicht von Westen, vor 1799
Unbekannter Künstler

Palais d'été de Greiz, vue de la façade ouest, avant 1799
Artiste inconnu

TO
HIS ROYAL HIGHNESS
GEORGE,
PRINCE REGENT
OF THE
UNITED KINGDOM OF GREAT BRITAIN AND IRELAND,
THIS WORK
IS
WITH ALL RESPECT AND HUMILITY
Dedicated,
BY HIS ROYAL HIGHNESS'S
MOST DEVOTED,
HUMBLE SERVANT,
GEORGE BROOKSHAW.

POMONA BRITANNICA;
OR,
A COLLECTION
OF
THE MOST ESTEEMED FRUITS
AT PRESENT CULTIVATED IN THIS COUNTRY,
TOGETHER WITH
THE BLOSSOMS AND LEAVES
OF SUCH AS ARE NECESSARY TO DISTINGUISH THE VARIOUS SORTS FROM EACH OTHER;
SELECTED PRINCIPALLY FROM
THE ROYAL GARDENS AT HAMPTON COURT,
AND THE REMAINDER FROM
THE MOST CELEBRATED GARDENS ROUND LONDON.
Accurately drawn and coloured from Nature;
WITH
FULL DESCRIPTIONS OF THEIR VARIOUS QUALITIES, SEASONS, &c.
BY
GEORGE BROOKSHAW, ESQ.

LONDON:
PRINTED FOR THE AUTHOR, BY R. BENSLEY, BOLT COURT, FLEET STREET;
...

Title page of the Pomona Britannica 1812
Titelblatt der Pomona Britannica 1812
Page de titre de la Pomona Britannica 1812

Botany and zoology, plant-breeding and gardening counted as worthy occupations among the English nobility.

Having herself illustrated a wide assortment of large-format works, now at Greiz, with very impressive flower and plant motifs, she must have particularly appreciated Brookshaw's publication. The aquatint etchings are naturalistic representations of the most popular English fruit varieties in subtle hues, satisfying not only high scientific and documentary standards, but also artistic ones as well. In this connection Elizabeth's loose sheets and albums containing studies of flowers and plants or butterflies and insects take on particular significance.

The *Pomona Britannica* was a fine acquisition for Elizabeth's library and collections. For her interests were not confined to history, literature, and art. Her strong interest in the natural sciences is documented by some herbals and manuscripts on natural history topics. Notes, essays and indexes on scientific findings and botanical terminology also exist, as well as instructions on berry and mushroom cultivation.

In retracing the ownership of the *Pomona Britannica*, we cannot but wonder how this book came into the possession of one of Germany's smallest states, the principality of Reuss with its seat at Greiz. After the death of the landgravine in 1840, a part of her dowry, and also her scientific papers and artwork, ultimately fell to her niece Karoline, daughter of Landgrave Gustav of Hesse-Homburg. This estate ought actually to have stayed in Homburg, but Karoline was married to the ruling prince Heinrich XX of the house of Reuss in 1839. Large portions of the estate, hitherto housed at Windsor Castle and Homburg, thus found their way around 1848 and thereafter, to the seat of the court at Greiz.

During the process of establishing a state archive in the Upper Castle, these hitherto hidden treasures of books, documents and copperplate engravings were rediscovered. The curator of the Dresden collection of copperplate engravings, Professor Hans W. Singer, was assigned the task of appraising the pieces of graphic art. According to his expert opinion, they constituted extraordinarily valuable books and graphic art collections. He even spoke of a new art Mecca in Germany. This moved the liberal-left republican government of Reuss in 1921 to set up the "Foundation of the Elder Line of the House of Reuss", following an amicable settlement with the representatives of the princely family. In the following year, finally, the English and Reussian estates, which had become state property, were transferred to the Summer Palace at Greiz, and the "State Collection of Books and Copperplate Engravings" was founded as soon as an extension of the building with the necessary installations was completed. From then on, the *Pomona Britannica* could be shown to the many interested visitors as a handsome showpiece of the collection.

Gotthard Brandler

kunstsinnige, naturwissenschaftlich gebildete und interessierte Königstochter war. Elizabeth hatte den Grundstock ihrer Sammlung Ende des 18. Jahrhunderts auf Schloss Windsor angelegt, besaß aber erst seit 1812 eine Apanage für private Bücher- und Kunstankäufe.

In den Kreisen des englischen Adels zählte im 18. und 19. Jahrhundert die Hinwendung zu Botanik und Zoologie, zu Pflanzenzucht oder Gartenkunst zu den hervorragenden Beschäftigungen. Als Buchkünstlerin, die eine ganze Reihe der in Greiz vorhandenen großformatigen Werke auf eindrucksvolle Weise mit Blüten- und Pflanzenmotiven illuminiert hatte, muss sie die Veröffentlichung von Brookshaw sehr geschätzt haben. Schließlich erfüllen die naturgetreuen, feinste Farbabstufungen erfassenden Aquatinta-Radierungen der beliebtesten englischen Fruchtsorten nicht nur einen hohen wissenschaftlich-dokumentarischen Anspruch, sondern es sind auch hervorragend gestaltete Kunstwerke. In diesem Zusammenhang erhalten auch Elizabeth' Studienblätter und Alben mit Darstellungen von Blüten und Pflanzen oder Schmetterlingen und Insekten eine besondere Bedeutung.

Die *Pomona Britannica* ergänzte gelungen den Bestand ihrer Bibliothek und Sammlungen. Denn ihre Interessen waren nicht nur historisch, literarisch und künstlerisch, sondern auch naturwissenschaftlich ausgerichtet. Dies belegen in ihrem Nachlass einige Herbarien und fachspezifische Manuskripte. So finden sich Notizen, Schriften und Verzeichnisse über wissenschaftliche Festlegungen und Termini zur Botanik sowie Unterweisungen zum Züchten von Beeren und Pilzen.

Wenn nun dem Weg der Eigentümerschaft der *Pomona Britannica* weiter nachgegangen wird, so stellt sich die Frage, wie denn dieses Buch ausgerechnet in den Besitz eines der kleinsten deutschen Fürstentümer, in die Herrschaft Reuss mit der Residenzstadt Greiz gelangen konnte. Nach dem Tode der Landgräfin Elizabeth im Jahre 1840 fiel letztlich ein Teil ihrer Aussteuer, dazu der wissenschaftliche und künstlerische Nachlass, an ihre Nichte Karoline, Tochter des Landgrafen Gustav von Hessen-Homburg. Dieser Nachlass sollte eigentlich in Homburg bleiben. Doch wurde Karoline 1839 mit dem regierenden Fürsten Heinrich XX. aus dem Hause Reuss vermählt. Große Teile der Hinterlassenschaft aus Windsor Castle und Homburg gelangten auf dem Erbschaftswege um 1848 und in den folgenden Jahren in die Residenzstadt Greiz.

Im Zuge der Einrichtung eines Staatsarchivs im Oberen Schloss entdeckte man dann die bislang verborgenen Schätze an Büchern, Dokumenten und Kupferstichen.

Mit der Einschätzung der Graphikbestände wurde der Kustos der Dresdner Kupferstichsammlung, Professor Hans W. Singer, beauftragt. Seinem Gutachten zufolge handelt es sich hierbei um außergewöhnlich wertvolle Bücher und Graphikkollektionen, so dass er sogar von einem neuen Kunst-Mekka in Deutschland sprach. Dies veranlasste die Regierung des linksliberal ausgerichteten Volksstaates Reuss, nach einem gütlichen Vergleich mit den Vertretern des Fürstenhauses 1921 die „Stiftung der Älteren Linie des Hauses Reuss" ins Leben zu rufen. Im folgenden Jahr wurde schließlich der in staatlichen Besitz übergegangene englische und reussische Nachlass in das Sommerpalais Greiz überführt und – nach einem Ausbau des Gebäudes mit der erforderlichen Einrichtung – die „Staatliche Bücher- und Kupferstichsammlung" begründet. Hier wurde fortan den zahlreichen interessierten Besuchern insbesondere auch die *Pomona Britannica* als ein Glanzstück der Sammlung vorgelegt.

Gotthard Brandler

cesse aussi cultivée dans les arts et les sciences de la nature. A la fin du XVIIIe siècle, Elisabeth avait déjà constitué la base de ses collections au château de Windsor mais ce n'est qu'à partir de 1812 qu'elle disposa d'un budget pour des achats privés de livres et d'objets d'art.

Dans les milieux aristocratiques anglais au XVIIIe et XIXe siècles, la botanique, la zoologie, la culture des plantes et l'art d'aménager les jardins étaient des occupations très prisées. Avec son talent d'enlumineuse, elle avait illustré de magnifiques motifs de fleurs et de plantes toute une série d'ouvrages de grand format conservés à Greiz, et à ce titre, elle avait certainement beaucoup apprécié la publication de Brookshaw. Car ses aquatintes des variétés de fruits anglais les plus prisés, à la fois si fidèles et si délicates dans les nuances, correspondaient parfaitement aux exigences scientifiques et documentaires de l'époque, tout en étant des œuvres d'art remarquablement bien conçues. Dans ce contexte, les feuilles d'étude et les albums d'Elisabeth, avec leurs représentations de fleurs, de plantes, de papillons et d'insectes, prennent évidemment elles aussi un sens particulier.

La *Pomona Britannica* complète superbement le fonds de livres d'Elisabeth et ses collections. Car, nous l'avons dit, cette princesse ne s'intéressait pas seulement à l'histoire, à la littérature et aux arts mais aussi aux sciences de la nature. En témoigne, dans sa succession, l'existence de quelques herbiers et manuscrits spécialisés, comprenant tout à la fois des notes, des textes, des répertoires de définitions scientifiques et de terminologies botaniques, ainsi que des instructions pour la culture des baies et des champignons.

A la recherche des différents propriétaires de la *Pomona Britannica*, on peut se demander comment il se fait que ce livre soit justement devenu la propriété de l'une des plus petites principautés d'Allemagne, la maison des Reuss, dans leur résidence de Greiz. Or, à la mort de la landgrave Elisabeth en 1840, une partie de sa dot ainsi que ses objets scientifiques et artistiques sont allés à sa nièce Caroline, fille du landgrave Gustave de Hesse-Hombourg. Les pièces de cette succession devaient en principe rester à Hombourg. Mais Caroline épousa en 1839 le prince régnant Henri XX de la maison Reuss. Ainsi, quantité de biens en provenance de Windsor Castle et de Hombourg parvinrent par voie d'héritage à la résidence de Greiz vers 1848 et dans les années qui suivirent.

C'est seulement en installant les archives nationales dans le Château supérieur, que l'on découvrit un trésor insoupçonné de livres, de documents et de gravures. L'évaluation des gravures fut confiée au conservateur de la collection d'estampes de Dresde, le professeur Hans W. Singer. L'expertise établit que les collections de livres et de gravures présentaient une valeur exceptionnelle. Singer parla même d'une nouvelle Mecque de l'art en Allemagne. Ceci incita le gouvernement libéral de gauche de l'état populaire de Reuss à créer en 1921, après un arrangement à l'amiable avec la maison princière, la «Fondation de la branche aînée de la maison Reuss». L'année suivante, l'héritage anglais et reussien, entre-temps devenu propriété de l'Etat, fut enfin transféré dans le Palais d'été de Greiz. Puis après avoir agrandi le bâtiment existant et l'avoir aménagé en conséquence, on créa la «Collection nationale de livres et de gravures». Cette collection suscita un vif intérêt et de nombreux visiteurs purent entre autres y consulter la *Pomona Britannica*, qui en est l'une des pièces les plus somptueuses.

Gotthard Brandler

Index of fruits | Verzeichnis der Früchte | Index des fruits

The numerals indicate page numbers | Die Ziffern verweisen auf die Seitenzahlen | Les chiffres renvoient aux numéros des pages

Allgemeines Teutsches Garten-Magazin, Weimar 1804–1817

Blütenpracht und Farbenzauber. Illustrated 18th and 19th-century plant-books from the collections of the Württembergische Landesbibliothek in Stuttgart. An exhibition on the occasion of the International Garden Show, Stuttgart 1993

Bertsch, Karl/Bertsch, Franz, *Geschichte unserer Kulturpflanzen*, Stuttgart 1947

Bischof, Herbert, *Großvaters alte Obstsorten*, Stuttgart 1998

Buchanan, Handasyde, *Nature into Art. A Treasury of Great Natural History Books*, London 1979

Desmond, Ray, *Dictionary of British and Irish Botanists and Horticulturists*, London 1994

Dlouhá, J., et al., *Obst*, Hanau 1995

Duhamel du Monceau, Henri Louis, *Traité des arbres fruitiers*, Paris 1768

Dunthorne, Gordon, *Flower & Fruit Prints of the 18th and 19th Centuries. Their History, Makers and Uses, with a Catalogue Raisonne of the Works in which they are found*, London 1970

Flowerdew, Bob, *Complete Fruit Book: A Definitive Source Book to Growing, Harvesting and Cooking Fruit*, London 1995

Forsyth, Wilhelm, *A Treatise on the Culture and Management of Fruittrees*, London 1802

Forsyth, Wilhelm, *Über die Kultur und Behandlung der Obstbäume*, Berlin 1804

Franke, Wolfgang, *Nutzpflanzenkunde. Nutzbare Gewächse der gemäßigten Breiten, Subtropen und Tropen*, Stuttgart 1989

Henrey, Blanche, *British botanical an horticultural literature before 1800. Comprising a history and bibliography of botanical and horticultural books printed in England, Scotland, and Ireland from the earliest time until 1800. Vol. II. The eighteenth century history*, London 1975

Kerner, Johann Simon, *Le Raisin, ses espèces et variétés, dessinées et colorées d'après nature*, Stuttgart 1803–1815

Knoop, Johann Hermann, *Pomologia*. 2 vols., Leeuwarden 1758–1763; German edition, Nuremberg 1760–1766

Koschatzky, Walter, *Die Kunst der Graphik. Technik, Geschichte, Meisterwerke*. 13th edition, Munich 1999

Lack, Eva/Lack, Hans Walter, *Botanik und Gartenbau in Prachtwerken*. With 9 colour plates and 44 reproductions, Berlin/Hamburg 1985

Lack, Hans Walter/Becker, Peter Jörg/Brandis, Tilo, *100 Botanische Juwelen. 100 Botanical Jewels*. Staatsbibliothek Preußischer Kulturbesitz (exhibition catalogue no. 30), Berlin 1987

Lechtreck, Hans-Jürgen, *Die Äpfel der Hesperiden werden Wirtschaftsobst. Botanische Illustration und Pomologie im 18. und frühen 19. Jahrhundert*, Munich/Berlin 2000

Lochner, Michael Friedrich, "Commentatio de Ananasa sive nuce pinea indica vulgo pinhas". In: *Continvation der Nuernbergischen Hesperidvm, Oder: Fernere gruendliche Beschreibung Der Edlen Citronat- Citronen- und Pomeranzen-Fruechte...; Benebenst einem Anhang von etlichen raren und fremden Gewaechsen / als Der Ananas / des Palm-Baums / der Coccus-Nuesse / der Baum-Wolle ... /* edited by Johann Christoph Volkamer, Nuremberg 1714

Lohwasser, Uta/Mäuser, Matthias, *Schöne Früchtchen*. Exhibition catalogue Naturkunde-Museum Bamberg, Bamberg 1999

McTigue, Bernard, *Nature illustrated. Flowers, plants, and trees. 1550–1900. From the Collections of the New York Public Library*. Preface by Eleanor Perényi, New York 1989

Miller, Philip, *The Gardeners Dictionary*. 1st edition. Vol. 1, London 1731; Vol. 2, London 1739

Miller, Philip, *Allgemeines Gärtner-Lexicon*. German edition, Nuremberg 1769

Morgan, Joan/Richards, Alison, *The Book of Apples*. With Paintings by Elisabeth Dowle, London 1993

Nissen, Claus, *Die botanische Buchillustration*. 2 vols. and supplement, Stuttgart 1951–1966

Ostertag-Henning, Karl-Ludwig, "Modellfrüchte – wächserne Kostbarkeiten der Pomologen", in: Zandera, *Mitteilungen aus der Bücherei des Deutschen Gartenbaus e. V.*, Vol. 15., No. 2, Berlin 2000

Pini, Udo, *Das Gourmet Handbuch*, Cologne 2000

Raphael, Sandra, *An Oak Spring Pomona. A selection of the rare books on fruit in the Oak Spring Garden Library*, Upperville Virginia 1990

Reichart, Thomas, *Die Ananas. Ein neues Weltwirtschaftsgut?*, Nuremberg 1982 (Nürnberger Wirtschafts- und sozialgeographische Arbeiten, Vol. 34)

Root, Waverley, *Food: An Authoritative and Visual History and Dictionary of the Foods of the World*, New York 1980

Schöne Dekore auf Meissener Porzellan. Photographs by Jürgen Karpinski, Zwickau 2001

Sickler, Johann Volkmar (ed.), *Der teutsche Obstgärtner*, Weimar 1794–1804

Störtzer, Mechtild, et al., *Steinobst*, Radebeul 1992

Taylor, Patrick, *100 englische Gärten. Die schönsten Anlagen des "English Heritage Parks and Gardens Register"*, Niederhausen 1997

Thurley, Simon (ed.), *The King's Privy Garden at Hampton Court Palace 1689–1995*, London 1995

Tietzel, Brigitte, *Fayence I. Niederlande, Frankreich, England*. Kunstgewerbemuseum der Stadt Köln, Cologne 1980

Photo credits | Bildnachweis | Crédits photographiques